1971

A BOOK OF COUNTRY THINGS

A BOOK OF
COUNTRY
THINGS

TOLD BY WALTER NEEDHAM
RECORDED BY BARROWS MUSSEY

THE STEPHEN GREENE PRESS
BRATTLEBORO, VERMONT · 1965

Map on page ix and portrait on page 1 by Robert MacLean.

Fifth Printing

Designed by R. L. Dothard Associates. Composition by Pioneer Printing Company. Printed in the United States of America.
Library of Congress catalog card number: 65-14693.

CONTENTS

RECORDER'S NOTE

"TOLD BY Walter Needham; recorded by Barrows Mussey": the words are carefully chosen. This story began as a stenographic transcription of what my neighbor remembered about his grandfather. The words are still his, rearranged and occasionally condensed, but nevertheless largely verbatim.

Anyone who takes this for a piece of ordinary ghost-writing "as told to" me will be much mistaken.

All I can claim is that I thought what he had to tell would fascinate country-dwellers, tinkerers, and nostalgic Yankees as much as it did me, if we could just get it on paper.

It's not every day you find someone who has practiced the accomplishments that went with log cabins (such as the one Gramp was born in in 1833), and who can explain them as if he were showing you how to saw and nail your first board. Since Vermont is the next-to-youngest New England state, life there a hundred and twenty years ago was probably much like that of Connecticut, say, in 1750. Walter Needham, through his grandfather, gives you a long look back.

I merely had the luck to live near him in Guilford, and the sense to ask questions.

A brief aside about the history of the manuscript: the first version was written just after I returned from duty with the Marine Corps in World War II, and part of it appeared in the *Saturday Evening Post;* but no book publication followed. I moved to Europe.

It then lay neglected and ultimately forgotten by its custodian at a learned society until Stephen Greene rediscovered it in the fall of 1964 and asked Walter Needham to bring it up to date. Nearly twenty years of added perspective may have served to make it the more unusual as a living voice from an American frontier that is gone, but that through Walter Needham's talk will perhaps be a trifle less soon forgotten.

Düsseldorf, Germany   BARROWS MUSSEY
January 1965

PEOPLE TALKED ABOUT

L. L. BOND, Walter Needham's maternal grandfather, was square as a brick—just dodge the sharp corners and you'd be all right.

WALTER NEEDHAM, raised by his grandfather to use his hands and his head.

JOHN GALE, lawyer, farmer, good friend; in later years the first citizen of Guilford, Vermont. His hobbies were local history and foiling nitwit schemes started by people who had no sense for the past.

GRANDMOTHER BOND, who died early. She never gave L. L. any arguments, but her suggestions always got followed.

EDWIN ADAMS of Marlboro, a champion sugarmaker who gave young Walter his first outside job.

JUDGE ROYALL TYLER, noted jurist and also the foremost native American writer of comedies and satirical novels, who came to Guilford in 1791 and later moved to nearby Brattleboro.

CLARENCE COOMBS, John Gale's and Walter Needham's neighbor, who is still a successful farmer on land acquired by his family more than a century and a half ago.

JANE GALE, John's mother. Her accomplishments included masterminding production of the Mineral Springs Distillery.

EPHRAIM GALE, John's grandfather, who ran the Liberty Pole Tavern around the time of the War of the Revolution.

FRANK BRASOR, who kept a store and gristmill in Algiers village, and lived to be a hundred years old.

VARIOUS early settlers, soldiers, Indians, blacksmiths, Welsh and Irish slate cutters, farmers, and typical Yankees who could turn their hands to most anything.

PLACES TALKED ABOUT

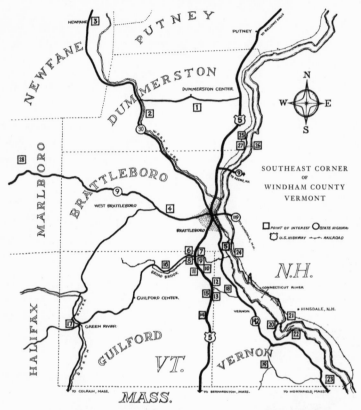

1. L. L. Bond birthplace
2. Granite quarry
3. County jail
4. Centerville
5. Fort Dummer (1724)
6. Blacksmith shop
7. Gristmill
8. Brasor's store
9. Gale place
10. Liberty Pole Tavern
11. Mineral Springs Distillery
12. Slate quarries
13. Slate quarries
14. Slate quarries

15. Needham place
16. Brandy Bridge
17. Covered bridge
18. Needham birthplace
19. L. L. Bond place
20. Vernon Dam
21. Fort Hill
22. Largest Indian lodge
23. Indian corn cellars
24. Indian burial ground
25. Indian relics
26. Houghton's Ferry
27. Eli Clark's house
28. Edwin Adams's farm

CHAPTER 1.

L.L. BOND
CO.i.16.VT.

Gramp

I WAS ALWAYS Grandpa's boy. He brought me up more than anyone else until I was a dozen years old. When I was sixteen I run away from home, and got as far as Indiana; afterward I come back. People sometimes ask me why I didn't go west and grow up with the country. I tell 'em, because Vermont is where I've been treated best, and oftenest.

Since I was sixteen I've always made my own living, never had a dollar from anyone, or ever owed anyone. I've been an automobile mechanic, and I've assembled electrical gadgets in a factory, but mostly I'm just an old Vermont Jack-of-all-trades.

My knowledge of doing things was from Gramp,

He was a
one-man education.

1

The first thing
to learn was
self-reliance.

from the way he done things. You see he lived in
the time when everything grew in the woods, and he
could make anything out of wood. When I come to
think back about Grandpa, I see that in his young days
he hardly bought anything except maybe from the
blacksmith. He was born in a log cabin; he was a
farmer all his life; they grew their own wool, and
dyed their own cloth, and made their own tallow
dips and their own ink, and cut their own quill
pens. They framed their own houses, and quarried
their own slate. An old Indian taught Grandpa about
medicinal herbs, and I still remember some of the
things he learned. This story is just going to be the
country things that he taught me; I think they'd ought
to be put down before they're forgotten altogether.

Gramp's name was Leroy L. Bond. I never knew
what the L. stood for; he was just L. L. He spent all
his life right in the two towns of Dummerston and
Vernon, one north of Brattleboro and the other south.
down in the southeastern corner of the state. We're
only five and a half hours by train from New York,
but I haven't been down there since I went to France
in 1917, and except in the Civil War I don't think
Gramp ever went much further away than Springfield.

Grandpa's parents put up a log cabin in Dummerston until they could build a house, and he was born
in that log cabin in 1833.

The schoolhouse was a log cabin too, maybe a
mile and a half away. I don't know what grade you
would say he got through, because he kept right on
until he was twenty-one, but he never went to school
except about three months in the winter. Everybody
around there did that in those days—just went to
school in the winter when they had time, and kept on
until they was twenty-one.

In later years I noticed he would never eat potatoes, specially not baked potatoes. I asked him why once. He told me that he lived in this log cabin up at a circular place in the hillside that they called the shoe of the mountain. In winter the cabin used to be so cold that he would have to get up and thaw out his cowhide boots in front of the fireplace before he went to school. He never had any gloves, so what he'd do, he'd put two potatoes in the ashes to bake. When his boots was thawed out and the potatoes was baked, he'd start for school with a hot potato in each hand. That way he kept his hands warm until he got to the schoolmaster's cabin; he'd keep his feet warm by running.

Holding hot potatoes.

Then the cold potatoes would be his lunch. He got pretty tired of them, for a steady diet.

Maybe some of the other boys used to do the same thing, because he told me potatoes wasn't worth more than ten cents a bushel in his day, and nobody wanted them at that price.

The remembrance of those cowhide boots must have stayed with him for the rest of his life, too. A pair of shoes seemed to be something he prized more than anything else; he just made a hobby of having boots and shoes. He always bought Congress shoes, with elastic in the sides, to give his feet a rest after all those years in cowhide. When the elastic wore out, he'd have to take a tuck in the sides of the

3

shoes, but he'd still be proud of them. He used to boast that he'd had one pair for four years. Either they'd have a tuck in them or maybe he wouldn't have worn them more than a few times, but anyway he was pleased that he could say he'd had them for four years.

That was always his way about anything he bought.

He always bought so as not to spend money.

I don't suppose he ever saw much more than a hundred dollars in cash from one year to another, but what he looked for when he bought anything was that it should be good. He didn't mind if it was expensive; it was the value for the money. This way he never *spent* money, he invested it.

I suppose this was partly because in his young days even what few things they did buy would be mostly in trade. Those cowhide boots he got so sick of, the cobbler would come to their house and live there while he fixed up all the boots and shoes for the family, and made whatever new ones was needed. Then he would move along to the next family. He kept this circuit going all the time. I guess the cobbler mostly brought his own hides, though people did tan their own. I've heard—I don't think it was from Gramp—that some of those old cobblers used to make boots that was straight up the back, not fitted around the ankle, and right and left foot just alike, interchangeable. Of course the shoes was all pegged with wooden pegs, not nailed.

Pretty much like Gramp.

I was born in 1896 in Vernon, which is a town on the Connecticut River right across from New Hampshire, and was settled in 1690, when it was a part of Northfield, Massachusetts. I'm like Gramp: the place I live now isn't but five or six miles from the house I was born in. He was my mother's father, and for some reason he and I got along good right from the start. I was his favorite grandchild. Most of them was afraid of him because he roared so. He hadn't much patience with his grandchildren or with anything else. He'd be working on something, and if it kept going wrong for more than a minute he was just as liable to let out a holler and throw the thing, and then start all over again.

I still remember how pleased I was one day when he was looking for the cover to the teakettle. At the time I thought it was kind of a shame that I didn't dare laugh, but maybe that's why I've never forgotten. Gramp filled the teakettle at the pump, and set the kettle on the stove, and then he looked around for the cover. He looked on the stove shelf, and he looked on the stove hearth, and he looked in the woodbox, and he looked in the sink, and then he went out and looked in the woodshed. By and by he begun to talk rather strong, wondering what he had done with the kettle cover.

I said, "You've got it right in your hand." He'd been carrying it everywhere he went.

He threw the teakettle cover on the floor, and stamped on it until he stamped it all out of shape.

I don't know why his roaring or anything never bothered me, but I just didn't mind at all. He used to make me things like a real Indian-fashion bow and arrow, and he taught me all the kinds of country work that I've always done. He used to give me ten cents once in a while to pull the weeds out of his onion patch and hoe potatoes and things like that, and specially to paint the cellar door.

His main object was to teach me how to do things, not so much to get the things done. About the first job he give me was to paint the cellar door. He mixed up some red ochre powder and oil, and told me to go down and get started.

How to work for somebody else.

5

I went downcellar, and looked at that door, and it had just had a fresh coat. So I come back up and told him the door didn't need painting.

He said, "I didn't ask you if the door needed painting or not; I told you to paint it. When you work for other people, do what they want, and not what you feel like doing yourself."

That's a thing some people just can't seem to learn, but thanks to Grandpa I've never had any trouble working for somebody else, not even in the army.

Off to save
the Union.

Maybe he had that a little in mind; when I was small he always called me Colonel. Of course I never knew the meaning of it until years afterward, and then I told him some time I was going to be in the war same as he was. He belonged to Company I of the Sixteenth Vermont Volunteers, from Dummerston, in the Civil War.

He said to me, "Don't you do it. You stay out of the army. But if you're ever drafted I'll disown you."

When he enlisted in 1862 he probably thought he was going in to kill Rebs, only they made him a cook instead. He was in the Battle of the Wilderness and the Battle of Gettysburg, but aside from that he spent most of the war looking for firewood. Once when he was laying in reserve, a solid cannon ball plowed

6

between him and the next man, and this next man says, "I never knew lightning to strike twice in the same place." So he rolls into the hole that the shot made, and in about a minute the next shot come over and dug up the place where he'd been lying.

I guess wars are quite a lot alike. The Sixteenth Vermont was pretty short of wood for the field kitchen most times, but they were only allowed to take the top rail off the fences for the fire. They'd take the top rail off a handy section. Then they'd go along again and take off the top rails again. When there was just one row of rails left along the ground, those was still the top rails, so they took them.

He was a very good cook in his later years, after my grandmother died, but I don't know whether he learned to cook from what they taught him in the army, or from doing the opposite. They had beans and pork for breakfast, and pork and beans for dinner, and beans and pork for supper. He said they mostly had pork and beans.

They weren't supposed to forage or steal any property off the country, but they did think it would be kind of nice if they could get hold of a turkey that was in the neighborhood. So the drummer went over to that farmyard in full uniform, drum and all. He cut a hole in the bottom head of his drum, and brought the turkey back into camp without getting caught. I don't know if Gramp ever had turkey dinner in the army but that once.

Drumming up their dinner.

So far as I could tell at my age, Grandpa knew everything; he was smarter than my father, in a way. If Gramp couldn't tell me, he could make a good story.

He told me one time they was on the railroad in some sort of a supply train. It was loaded so heavy that the old locomotive could only just about draw it;

7

and the Rebels was after them with another train on the same track. The old engine was just staggering along, and by and by the Rebels begun to catch up. They about decided they was going to lose their supplies—they'd have to abandon the train and take to the woods. Then one fellow got the idea that he could hold the Rebels off. He run up to the engineer, and borrowed his oil can, and then he hung off the back platform. Just as the trainload of Rebels come tooting along around a bend this fellow begun oiling the rails. The Rebels couldn't get no traction, and Gramp's crowd pulled clean away from them.

It all added up to victory.

The only other close shave that Gramp used to tell me about was near Gettysburg, but not in the battle. He said the mosquitoes there was terrible big. They was pretty thick one night after supper, and an extra big swarm of them come at him, so he tipped the bean kettle over, and got under it. He had the big iron ladle in his hand. He set there under the kettle, and the mosquitoes begun drilling through to get at him. As their bills would come through the kettle, he'd clinch them over with the ladle. When he'd clinched over enough of them, they couldn't pull out, and the mosquitoes just flew off with the kettle.

When I was little I never knew whether Gramp really meant his stories, or was just stuffing me.

I have the impression that Gramp used to go hunting quite a lot, and I know that he used to catch game with deadfalls, snares, and yank-ups, which are snares on a larger scale. Deadfalls and snares are against the law now.

By the time I knew him, he had three guns: an old smoothbore musket that was pretty much of a relic, a muzzle-loading double-barreled shotgun, and a great clumsy thing that used to be a flintlock when

8

it was carried during the War of the Revolution, and he called the Queen's Arm. Right down to this day, I can't hardly think about Gramp without remembering a yarn he told me about his shotgun.

He said he figured on going hunting, so he put in two charges of powder. When he come to look for his shot, he found he'd used it all up, and he didn't want to take the trouble of getting out his bronze bullet mold and casting more. He scratched around in the shop, and happened on a box of tacks. He shook some of the tacks into one barrel, but tacks was kind of scarce too, and he didn't want to use them all. He saw an old broken jackknife lying around, and he just dropped that down the other barrel.

Then he took a turn around the woods, but he didn't see a thing. He walked right around the north pasture, and up through the woodlot, and nary a sign of game. Finally he got disgusted, and started home through the sugarbush.

Still more double-barreled improvising.

And then right next to the sugarhouse a rabbit set up on its hind legs and looked at him. He got ready to shoot, and just as the rabbit dropped down, he fired.

He fired the barrel with the knife in it first. The knife was so heavy that it went low, and split the rabbit's skin right down the middle. The skin

9

flapped open and flew up just as he fired the other barrel, with the tacks. Those tacks spread the hide neat and tight on the back wall of the sugarhouse.

Some magazine printed this story a few years back, but Gramp told me about it when I was six, before the magazine was ever thought of.

I don't know why he didn't treat his pear tree with the shotgun; maybe it was part of his plan to teach me. Anyway, this pear tree grew very thrifty, only it wouldn't bear. It was a real handsome tree, but there just wasn't any pears.

One day Grandpa gave me a hammer and some pieces of old cut nails, and told me to go and drive them in the tree all around.

I asked him if it wouldn't spoil the tree. He said no, I could drive in all I'd a mind to.

I pounded away until I was tired. Afterward I found out that the reason was to retard the growth of the tree. It was all going to wood, and Grandpa figured that driving in nails would kind of kill it all around, and make it grow pears instead of new wood.

There isn't any point to this story, because I don't know if the tree ever bore or not.

If it didn't, though, it was nearly the only thing Gramp ever couldn't get to grow right. Until his last years he used to grow most of his own tobacco for smoking and chewing. He liked to smoke either a clay pipe or some old pipe that had been burned and charred. To light it he would poke a live coal into the ashes, and pick it up with his bare fingers, and put it in his pipe. The pipe bowl always used to be charred from the hot coal on top. When he was a boy they used flint and tinder; by my time they had the old brimstone matches that they used to call eight-day matches because you'd strike one and

Lighting a pipe the easy way.

have to wait eight days before the sulphur would burn off, otherwise you'd have a mouthful of brimstone instead of smoke. Gramp said a pipe always tasted much better lit with a coal than with an eight-day match.

He used to make his own chewing tobacco, too. He would take a chunk of black birch and bore a hole in it. Then he would pull the big veins out of the

tobacco leaves, and cram the rest of the leaf down in the hole he had bored. He would punch the tobacco down, and pour in a few drops of the maple molasses that collects when you scoop a hollow in maple sugar and let it stand for a while. Then he would put in some more tobacco leaf, and pound that down hard, and put in a few more drops of maple molasses. Finally he'd have the auger hole pounded pretty full, and he'd whittle a tight-fitting plug, and drive it in just as hard as he dared. Then he would set the block of green birch away. The longer it aged, the better it was; probably he'd leave it until the wood got dry.

His recipe for a good chew.

When he wanted a chew of tobacco, he would split open the birch block, and a big long cylinder of tobacco would come out. He would slice it off, one chew at a time.

I don't know whether he preferred homemade things because they was all he could get, or whether he really decided they was better. The only thing I have to go by is the time his store-built galluses broke. While he was repairing them he told me about the galluses his mother knit for him when he was a young fellow. He went over with his father and a couple of his brothers to look at a piece of land. They decided to clear it, stump it out, fence it, and plow it up.

There was a big oak tree grew in the middle. He said this oak tree was so crooked that a squirrel could run right around the tree through the crooks, and you couldn't ever see it. They cut the oak tree, and used it for fencing. The fence they made was so crooked that when they pastured hogs, the hogs would crawl out through the fence, and find they were still inside the lot.

When Great-Grandfather and the boys come to plow the lot, they hitched one yoke of old oxen ahead of a couple of yoke of young steers. This was along into the late spring when the flies begun to bother and bite, and the steers was rather frisky. There was quite a lot of backing up and pulling and hauling and one thing and another; the oxen got tired of it, and finally they bolted.

The yarn that stretched crosslots.

Gramp's brothers and his father didn't try to stop them, but just let them run. They ran crosslots, and Gramp thought he'd hold them back by driving the plow into the ground. The oxen pulled it right along, and it hit the oak stump in the middle of the field, and plowed clear through the stump.

The stump snapped together and caught the seat of Gramp's pants, and Gramp held all three yoke of oxen right there, and his knit galluses never let go.

From what you hear nowadays, you might think that an old Yankee farmer like Grandpa would be a great hand for prayers and churchgoing. He did get

a lot of fun out of church, but it wasn't from attend-
ing, because he never did. Just once I remember of
his going to a prayer meeting; the leading spirit was
a spinster lady. He went to sleep during the services.
After the meeting people begun to leave, and the
stirring around woke him up, and this old maid asked
him if he had got right with Jesus. He kind of
smothered a yawn, and told her, "Jesus? I don't know
as I ever had any trouble with Him."

On the other hand he always read the Bible every
night. He could quote book, chapter, and verse on
almost any subject. I never knew just why he had
such a craze for the Bible, but maybe it was to help
him in his great hobby.

His chief entertainment was to bother some young
minister and get him turned around. As soon as the
minister would say anything, Gramp would jump
on him with a quotation from the Bible. He used to
refrain from going to every church in Dummerston,
Putney, Brattleboro, Guilford, and Vernon, but he
did love to meet the new minister. It was rather a
shock to Grandmother, because she was a very stiff-
backed Puritan Christian woman, and his talk used to
kind of get her riled up. But she never said much
about it, because there wasn't no use, it would just
provoke him all the more. I think eventually she
must have learned it was time for her to leave the
room if she couldn't get the minister out before
Grandpa asked whether the parson really believed
that Jonah swallowed the whale.

Invariably the minister would say, "Why, of course.
Scripture tells us so."

And then Gramp would look disgusted, and say,
"Well, you must be a durn fool. No man could eat
a whale."

CHAPTER 2.

On the Farm

PEOPLE THAT AREN'T FARMERS don't know what the word *season* means. About all they notice is if it's warm or cold, and if they have to wear overshoes, and in Vermont maybe if the trees are turning bright red in the fall.

Grandpa done everything by the seasons. The first thing you do that you might enjoy during the year in Vermont begins the fore part of March. You start getting ready for sugaring.

Looking to his sugar tools.

Gramp would go over all his sap buckets, and wash them, and drive the hoops tight. You'll see later how he made all his own buckets and tubs. When the buckets and tubs and spouts and kettle was all washed, he'd

14

stack them outside ready to load on the sledge when
the weather turned. If the snow was deep, he'd have to
break out the roads in the woods. He would drive
around over them with the oxen, and wallow out the
trail, and shovel out the drifts. He worked everything
with oxen; horses was too fast for him.

Breaking road and tapping.

Then he and my uncles would throw the buckets
off by the trees. Later on they would come back to
tap the trees and hang the buckets.

Sugaring would last up to the first or middle part
of April, according to how the season carried on.

Mud time comes after sugaring. City people mostly
think Vermont is frozen up tight all winter and then
the moment it gets warm you can come out of your
cave. The truth of the matter is that Gramp got
around a good deal when the snow was hard, and
if he was snowed in he found things to do in the
barn. But in mud time there's just nothing you can
do except mend fences.

The same warm weather that brings the frost out of
the ground starts the buds and slows the maple sap
way down, and for most of April you have to rassle
in wet, sticky black mud up to your knees if you go
out at all. I don't know but what it's worse now, with
automobiles, than it was in Grandpa's day. Sometimes they have to close schools in mud time, where
during a blizzard they just put more men on the snow-
plows.

Mud or no mud (and I never seen an April when
there wasn't mud), you have to get your fences mended
by the second week in May at least, and some years
by the first week. That is turning-out time: you turn
out the cattle to pasture after the long winter in
the barn.

I can't say I ever enjoyed building fences myself,
and I think Gramp took more pride in the way he

15

could build a stone wall, but fences was a study all by themselves around here before wire come into use.

There was the old pole fence, and the stake-and-rider, and the zigzag rail fence, and the posthole fence.

One-pole fence.

The simple pole fence was quite common around Vernon, where I was born and Gramp lived in his later years. You drove two stakes in the ground to make an X, and a little farther on another pair, as far as you wanted to go. You just laid a pole across from one X to another, and you had a level one-rail fence.

The stake-and-rider took more poles, but it was harder to break through. You drove your two stakes to make an X, the same as for a pole fence. Then you laid a pole in the X, but you let the far end rest on the ground. You drove another X *over* this pole about halfway along, and laid another pole on that,

with its far end on the ground; and so on all around the pasture. It's a bristly-looking thing, with the poles

Stake-and-riders.

all slanting in one direction, and the top ends supported in the X's. Back in the hills around Gramp's old homestead in Dummerston they always used stake-and-rider.

Before that, though, Gramp had often made stump fences. When you first cleared a new field, you would go with the oxen to stump it out. You would dig

around a stump until you found a big root that run
out sideways; you would hitch to the root, and lead
your chain across the top of the stump to your yoke
of oxen on the other side. When you started the
oxen, the stump would turn over as it came out.
Then you dragged them to the border of the field
and turned them up on their side; it made a fence
and got the stumps out at the same time. Even though
this was the first kind of fence, there's still some of the
stumps left around the fields in Vernon.

Stumping out.

Vernon had mostly rail fences, though. A rail fence
goes in zigzags, as if it was a snake wiggling. Gramp
used to make them out of the long, straight chestnut
rails that grew in Vernon. For a foundation he would
put down two round stones, one on top of the other,
which he called the hub. If you just put one stone
under a fence or a wooden foundation, the moisture
creeps up the stone, and rots the wood. With two
stones the moisture doesn't crawl up the second stone.

Gramp would lay two hubs twenty foot apart, then
a third one in the middle outside the direct line
between number one and number two, to make an
angle, and add a fourth one beyond the second hub,
at the same angle. He would put a rail from one to
three, and a rail from two to four; then, to get his
build, he'd put a third rail from two back to three,

Two-stone hubs
for zigzag rails.

17

setting it across the ends of the first two rails. He kept laying hubs and adding rails until he got the length and height he wanted, with the rails interlocking at the hubs like the corners of a log cabin. Naturally if he hadn't made the hub like he did, the bottom rail would have rotted out, and that would have been the hardest to replace in a snake fence.

Occasionally the top rail might blow off in a high wind, but in general I think the old rail fence was the longest-lived one of all. John Gale, the man I learned most from next to Gramp, had a manure shed just beyond his house, and back of that shed until about a year ago was a few sections of rail fence, where it turns the corner on the pasture line. John Gale's grandfather built that fence over a hundred and twenty-five years ago.

The reason these fences was so plentiful in Vernon was because of the great chestnut forests. Vernon had just about the biggest stand of chestnut in the United States before the blight killed it all off. You still see enormous, dead, white chestnuts all through the woods there. The main use of the chestnut in my time was for railroad ties; any man who owned a chestnut lot had a steady income just cutting ties. Chestnut is a sort of a weed tree; it grows real fast.

Why chestnut made good fencing. It made good fence rails because it split so readily. It grew tall and straight, and lots of times you could get two or three twelve-foot lengths from one tree without any knots. It was straight grained, and if you started to split it down the center it would run along the whole length just as nice as you please.

Posthole fences. A posthole fence was something fancy, for the barnyard or in front of the house. Grandpa never made very many of them. You set up a row of posts, each one with two or three holes going right through, and you slipped the ends of the rails into these holes.

18

The same idea, only with bigger holes, made bar-posts for a barway. Gramp had a special posthole axe, like a fireman's axe with a very narrow bit, only the blade wasn't so rounded. You could chop the holes right through the post with this axe. You split the posts in half first, to get a flat side that you could work on.

I bet these politicians that you read about would rather mend their political fences than any part of Gramp's pasture fence.

After turning-out time came the ordinary spring work: plowing, harrowing, and planting. That was very particular work with Gramp, because his greatest pride was his garden and his crops, specially his corn. His corn come first, and then his garden had to look just so, with the rows perfectly straight and the potatoes hoed exactly right.

When he put me to dropping potatoes, instead of dropping them I had to plant them. He gave me a stick so that I could measure from one hill to the next. If I asked how big he wanted the hill, he always said, "Make it big enough to hold a half-bushel of potatoes." You have no idea what a lot of dirt that takes. Not that he ever expected to get so many potatoes, but he just liked to be sure.

Next came planting time.

You think of the ordinary farmer as kind of careless about the look of things, but Gramp wasn't like

19

that. As I say, all the rows had to be as straight as a string, and he made me take a ruler to the potatoes even though he wouldn't eat them after they was grown; and besides that, he always raised a few cucumbers just because they grew pretty, and he liked to see them grow. He wouldn't eat them either, because he said the hogs wouldn't touch them, and he wouldn't eat anything a hog wouldn't eat. All he got out of them was the satisfaction, and if anybody came along that wanted any, they could have some.

All his crops must be hoed by hand before the fifteenth of June, because that was the start of haying. Unless the haying is done before the first of August, it's practically no use; it's no good after that. The hay is too ripe, just gone to seed, mostly fiber, and hardly worth cutting. There's no real food value to it by then.

Gramp was supposed to march in the parade and see the rest of the boys on Decoration Day, but that wasn't so much of a celebration as the Fourth of July. The Fourth was a great day.

At four o'clock on the morning of the Fourth of July was always the first blast with the old Queen's Arm. The Queen's Arm was a gun Grandpa had that he always told me was used by the Hessians who came over here with Burgoyne. It had a big crown stamped on the barrel, to show it was British army ordnance; that's why he called it the Queen's Arm, after Queen Victoria—even though it came from back in the time of King George the Third. It had been rebuilt from a flintlock to percussion lock, and it used caps that looked like little stovepipe hats. The Queen's Arm had a queer-looking butt—the part you put against your shoulder looked awful small compared to the clumsiness of the whole gun.

Relic from the Revolution.

20

Gramp's explanation was that when the British troops shot it, it was much longer and heavier, and they put the butt under their arm. They never fired from the shoulder, but held it breast-high and just pointed it in the general direction. Our soldiers' guns were lighter, even though they were long, too, and we sighted them from the shoulder, so our fire was more effective. This helped a lot with the outcome. When the Queen's Arm was made over, the main part of the butt was cut off short enough to put against a man's shoulder. Gramp always shot it by holding it crossways over his head and firing it off.

They pointed, but we sighted.

Possibly the Queen's Arm came from somebody like the white-haired old man I once heard about that they had on the platform at an election rally over in York State during the Harrison Hard-Cider Campaign of 1840. They used to like to get war veterans up on the platform in those days the same as they did in Gramp's time and my time. The orator give a long story about how this old fellow had risked his life for liberty in '76, and now he was ready to cast his vote for it. The crowd was real pleased, but the speaker couldn't leave well enough alone, he had to ask the old fellow if he hadn't fought in that great

21

struggle. "Yass," says the old fellow with a German brogue, "I vas in de var." "And now, my venerable friend," says the speaker, "who was your commander in the noble battle for independence?" "Cheneral Burgoyne," the old fellow said.

The Queen's Arm must be fired during the day, once for each of the states we had then, and as many more times as you could find an excuse for. There could be one for the President, one for the State of Vermont, and one for the Governor, or for most anything, but mostly for the fun of it.

The Queen's Arm was a muzzle-loader, of course, and it had an iron ramrod. I read somewhere once that Frederick the Great, King of Prussia, won all his wars mostly because he introduced iron ramrods. Gramp's old Civil War smoothbore had a hickory ramrod. I asked Gramp which kind was best, and he agreed with the King of Prussia.

He told me the iron ramrod was far better than the wooden one because when the wild pigeons used to come through, he would sneak up on them, and instead of taking the ramrod out he would leave it in the gun. When he found a row of pigeons sitting on a limb, he could shoot the whole row of them at once, and have them skewered on the iron ramrod.

Gramp's Civil War musket was more like the Queen's Arm than what it was like the rifle I carried in France. The cartridge was a little paper tube; the bullet went in first, and the powder went on top of the bullet. When they wanted to load, they would bite off the end of the cartridge, and drop the powder down the barrel. The paper cartridge and the bullet was rammed down on top. There was a special military way to grasp the ramrod and twirl it in your fingers and shoot it down the barrel three times by the numbers, catch it on the rebound, twirl it in the air, and put it back in its place under the barrel. Then they capped the gun and was ready to fire.

They didn't get much accuracy or range that way. With Gramp's own gun that he used for sporting, he would fire about a one-ounce ball, with a patch to make the ball fit tight in the bore. Sometimes he would use a cross patch, a piece of cloth shaped like a Maltese cross. A grease patch was still better. If you wanted to increase the range even more, you would spit on the patch, and make a wet patch.

Making patches and bullets for hunting.

Gramp used to cast his own bullets of course, from bar lead that was brought in from Boston or Hartford, since there is but little lead in these parts. There is a vein in the town of Westminster, but it must be small; no one has worked it as I know of, though I've been told it runs about twenty percent silver, so it would make fine bullets. There is also said to be lead in the mountain across the Connnecticut from Brattleboro, where the Indians dug it for their muskets. They kept its location secret. A friend of mine claimed he found it, but he has never been able to find it again.

The Queen's Arm blew up one Fourth of July, and blew about a foot off the end of the barrel. Gramp almost cried when the Queen's Arm was spoiled.

The other thing Gramp had to have to make a real Fourth of July was new potatoes and green peas from his garden. This was the one time of year that he enjoyed potatoes, and I suppose even that was mainly a matter of pride in his garden.

There was generally a chicken dinner or something a little special, but his favorite was roast pork. Along with the new potatoes and green peas he would have new bread, baking-powder bread baked in a round pan like a cake. He preferred it to bakers' bread; they begun to have commercial bread in his later years, but he wouldn't ever touch it.

Somehow haying always seemed to last all summer. Haying was too big a job for one farmer alone; there was no mowing machines, and they all mowed by hand. They would have mowing bees, and later in the year husking bees, to get the work done.

The man that got his haying done first always shouldered his scythe and fork, and started down the road to the next man. He would start in there, and when he finished that up he would go on to the next man. There wasn't much of any money in it; it was just a neighborly thing to do. A man would get his board, and his neighbor would help him out with *his* haying.

At one time Gramp was the champion mower of Dummerston with both a scythe and a cradle. The cradle is for grain, and has a set of long wooden fingers set parallel to the blade of the scythe; it catches the grain so you can spread it to one side. Gramp won the Dummerston scything championship in a contest to see who could mow a given distance in a certain time with a perfect swath. They had judges to see that the swath was perfectly even. Two men would start on a level, probably ten feet apart, and mow their way up the left side of the field; then at the far end they would turn to the right and mow across the end, then turn to the right again and mow

Setting up a scything contest.

24

their way back. If the inside man could "mow the other man out of his swath" by getting to the end of the field first, so that the outside man couldn't turn to the right without crossing the inside man's swath, then the inside one was a pretty good man. I don't believe anyone ever mowed Grandpa out of his swath.

Cutting a swath to win.

In his day they would go out about four o'clock in the morning, calculating to mow a couple of acres before breakfast. Two or three men with the long scythe that they used in those days, cutting an eight-foot swath, would mow more than the average farmer could now with a pair of horses.

Gramp told me once about some fellow that stopped at a place and asked for a job to help with the haying. The farmer says, "Well, I've got about all the help I need."

"Yes," the fellow says, "you've got some good men there, but what they need is a leader. I'm a leader when it comes to mowing."

"Well," the farmer says, "I don't know but what I will hire you. I guess probably they do need a little punching up some way."

The other fellows heard it or got wise to it somehow, so when he started to lead, they all let out on him, and mowed him out of his swath. Along toward noon, when they got ready to leave, the farmer come down to look them over, and the new fellow was behind; he was the last man on the end. "Well, what happened to you? I thought you was a leader."

"Now I'll tell you," the fellow says, "I did think that was what they needed. But I finally concluded that what they needed was a driver."

Gramp first taught me to mow when I wasn't hardly big enough to hold up the scythe. I stood in front of him, and hung on to the nibs, as he called them, that is, the handgrips of the scythe. He swung the scythe,

25

and kicked me in the heels, first one, then the other, to tell me how to step. If you don't step out just right as you swing, you won't make any progress; you simply stand in one place. You learn the rhythm so that you step exactly so far each time, and swing exactly so far with each step.

Hold it right, keep the rhythm, and whet it toward the cutting edge.

While I was catching on to that, Gramp kept telling me to keep the heel of the scythe down. The ordinary fellow that starts to mow, he generally sticks the point of the scythe in the ground because he don't keep the heel down. So long as you get the rhythm and keep the heel down, you can mow right along. The first day Grandpa taught me, I was really too little to manage the scythe, but when I got to be ten or a dozen years old, and tried mowing alone, I got along all right, even if I did have to hold the scythe up nearly shoulder high.

Nothing you learn to do in the country is any good if you can't take care of the tools. Gramp started right in teaching me to sharpen a scythe. Grinding a scythe on a grindstone has to be done just so. You must always grind in the right direction. You don't grind at right angles; you grind diagonal toward the cutting edge and toward the heel. If you do it any other way it don't cut, that's all; it just slides over the grass. If

you look at what you think is a sharp, keen scythe under a glass, you'll see that it has little ragged teeth, like saw teeth, all hooking toward the point of the blade. As you swing your scythe through the grass, these teeth catch the straws, and actually saw them off.

When you're whetting the scythe by hand with a stone, one of those small ones shaped like a corncob, you still have to be careful that you don't never draw the whetstone toward the back edge of the scythe. The ridge near the back edge of the scythe is there

26

to guide the stone, so that you can keep an even bevel.

Not all modern tools are better than the old ones. The only kind of snath—scythe handle—that you can get now is ash, bent around jigs in a factory. Gramp always used a steam-bent, black-cherry snath, and I wish I could get one now. They used to bend them by hand somewhere upcountry, Danby, I think. The cherry was bent so that when you took hold of the nibs you just naturally held your arms up, and the scythe went around to position of its own accord. The ash is harder to bend than cherry, and I never seen an ash snath yet that was really bent to suit me. And then, the cherry was lighter, and had more life to it; it was more springy. The ash has a kind of a dead feeling; there's no give to it.

The black-cherry snaths they used to have were better bent.

I don't know why they give up making cherry snaths, unless because the cherry was selected stuff and hard to get in quantity.

Right after the haying come the cutting of oats. Then along in September Gramp would dig his potatoes and cut his corn. By the first of October the corn should be stooked and the potatoes and oats all in.

Grandpa's house set down right on the ground like all old-fashioned houses, but some time after it was built he dug a small cellar, with a hole so that you could get in from outside, to put the potatoes in.

When they dug potatoes, they would go out with the oxcart, and take forks instead of potato hooks like you use now. They run the forks right under the hills of potatoes, and picked them up with a shake. Anything that would stay on the fork they would pitch into the cart. The ox would plod along as they went, and occasionally he would get into the weeds and have to be straightened out. They would keep pitching potatoes until they got them all.

Then they went around and backed the ox toward the cellar entrance, and tipped the cart up, and kicked the potatoes downcellar with their boots.

They would turn the pigs out into the fields, and let them eat up what was left, what you would have to bend your back for.

Besides the other crops, Grandpa always raised some choice beans.

Beans pollinate quite easily, and naturally Gramp was always finding different-colored beans in his bean field. He'd plant all white beans, but every so often some would come up red-speckled, or black-eyed, or other different colors. One particular fall when he was threshing the beans on the barn floor, he found quite a number of sports. He decided he would save all these pretty ones for seed, so he squatted down and went to work with a little tin dish. It took a considerable time to pick over his whole season's bean crop, but finally he did get most of the multicolored beans picked out.

As he got up, he tipped over the dish. He patiently picked them all up again, which was doing good, for him; then he stood up with the dish and looked around to see if he had got the last ones. And he spilled them again.

The last of them special seed beans was when he threw the empty dish out through the barnyard.

Through November, the rainy season, come husking time. He always did the husking in his leisure time, stripping the ears of corn and putting them in the crib.

Rainy season into snow time.

Thanksgiving was in Grandmother's scope—a regular good old-fashioned feast, and generally the whole family arriving from everywhere—aunts, uncles, cousins, grandchildren, and all. The old rooster had to get the axe, and it was a pretty wild time, but it was more Grandmother's than Grandpa's.

Then it come time to cut wood. He would chop right along into the winter until the snow got too deep. He generally calculated to get the trees cut before he was snowed in, and then he could saw them up by hand with his old bucksaw with its homemade frame and a rawhide thong tightener. He would split the wood and pile it up in the shed. I used to have a

29

Wood in the shed, but no cider for Gramp.

big part in that. I'd pile, and he'd split. Then I'd saw some, and he'd split. I can tell you I had to pile that firewood just so, all sawed ends out, absolutely straight and smooth all the way up, no chopped ends or peaked sticks showing anywhere. It must be done very nicely in a workmanlike manner.

That's one of the few things where I ever disagreed with Gramp. To this day I think the wood would have dried faster and burned better if we'd just thrown it into the shed, with natural air spaces all through.

October and November was always cider time around here, but for some reason Gramp never cared much for cider. Vermont had a temperance law when I was a boy, mostly on account of cider. Hard cider makes people awful mean when they're drunk, and these choppers used to go out in the woods with a jug of hard cider in the late fall. They'd get to quarreling, and cut each other up with their axes. For a long time after they passed the Vermont prohibition law, there was a big decline in axe murders.

But Gramp wasn't much of a drinking man, and the only thing he done with his apples was to put them downcellar. He would bring them out all winter long to feed the cattle. He would sort the apples, and take the spotty ones out to the cattle. I don't suppose he got a dollar's worth of apples to eat all winter.

Christmas wasn't much more than just another day to Grandpa. He generally would have a Christmas dinner, and a new bottle of Van Horn gin. The bottle would last him about six months. He would fill a little glass about half full with two tablespoons of maple sugar (or white sugar, in later years), and pour some gin in on top of that. His drink would be about a teaspoonful, mainly for his cough.

When the snow finally did get too deep, and he couldn't go out, he would do his flailing and clean up his grain.

He would sweep the barn floor, and put down what was called the flooring, a layer of rye or oats about a foot deep.

He would flail that. After it had been all threshed, it had to be shook up and turned over with a fork and flailed again.

Next he pitched off the straw, and then took his winnowing tray, which was a boxlike affair with hand holes on the sides and no end or top. He would take the grain in that, and get a shaking motion to it that blew the chaff practically all out. To winnow beans he used to wait for a windy day, and take them out and pour them from one tub to another while the wind blew the dirt away. It saved a lot of work.

A flail is made of two parts. I guess there's people nowadays that haven't ever seen a flail. The handle is called the stave, and varies in length according to the fancy of the man that uses it. The swingel (sometimes you see it called swingle), the part that strikes the grain, is not more than two feet long. You change it according to the grain you're threshing. For oats you use a heavy swingel; for beans you have to have a light one, because the heavy ones would crush the

beans. The swingel is hinged loose to the stave. Sometimes this would be done with a wooden swivel, a thin splint bent into a bow and lashed on over the end of the swingel, and another bow lashed over the end of the stave. Those are unusual, though. The most prized fastening was an eelskin; if you couldn't get eelskin, it was woodchuck rawhide.

The swingel has to turn both ways because you strike both right and left. We always started striking left, two of us standing up side by side. I'd swing my stave over and bring the swingel down on the grain to the left, and Gramp would swing and bring his down about six inches from mine. Then I would bring my flail up over my left shoulder, and down to the right, and he would hit about six inches away again. You just keep your ears folded back and don't hit yourself in the head, and you're all right.

After we had gone the length of the barn floor once, we took forks, as I said before, and shook the flooring and turned it over other side up, and flailed the other side. Then it was supposed to be all out. We would shake it up again, pitch the straw off, and sweep the oats to one side to be winnowed.

And then it would be nearly time to think about sugaring again.

CHAPTER 3

Sugaring

SUGARING is one kind of country work that is done better now than it was in Grandpa's time. At least we think so; Gramp might have concluded that it wasn't worth the extra trouble and expense.

Nowadays the State of Vermont has an official grading system; they have a case with little jars of syrup, ranging from fancy, which is practically colorless, down to C, which is dark like molasses. You match your own syrup against the standard colors. It also has to weigh just so much per gallon.

You can't hardly sell the fancy grade outside of Vermont; it's so clear and fine that New York people

Too good to be real.

think it must be mostly cane syrup. I've seen New York people stop at roadside stands around here and have the most awful arguments because they claimed they knew genuine Vermont maple syrup when they seen it.

I don't know if I ought to admit this, because to most people Vermont and maple is the same thing, but there's a lot of maple syrup made in New Hampshire, Canada, upper York State, Pennsylvania, Ohio, and even West Virginia and Wisconsin. They'll ship some of it to Vermont just so it can be put up under a Vermont label. Some of the commercially made stuff from St. Johnsbury and Burlington does have part cane syrup mixed in, and for my part they can keep that stuff they make in West Virginia. But I will say that Vermont syrup made by a good man in a good sugar year is pretty hard to beat.

Maple to Gramp was a tub of dark sugar in the back pantry, and he hunked it out when he wanted some sweetening.

Grandpa wouldn't hardly have known what I was talking about. In the first place he never used syrup, he used sugar. Hard sugar he could keep; it didn't take as much space, and it didn't ferment. If he should want syrup, all he had to do was melt the sugar up, and if he wanted it thinner, just add water. He hardly ever bothered, though, because what little syrup he wanted would collect of its own accord after he scooped some sugar out of the tub. And even as late as when I was a boy they never paid no attention to color at all. Whatever it was, they didn't know any difference—it was just sugar. They never produced fancy sugar until the time of the evaporators, which were just beginning to come around when I was a boy. I can remember when the syrup was always black as molasses. Now they can't sell that kind except to be used for curing tobacco.

I imagine Grandpa would always have preferred white sugar if he could have got it. It was a rarity in

Vermont when he was young; when he was old, and living royally, for him, on his Civil War pension, I know he used white sugar.

Like I said, they generally start sugaring operations along the first week in March: they begin to wash the buckets. Nowadays they get the buckets out of the sugarhouse, and scald them. In Grandpa's time they didn't have sugarhouses to begin with, and at first they didn't even keep buckets from year to year, but made wooden trenchers.

Making trenchers to catch the sap.

They would cut down a white birch or some other tree with soft wood, and split the tree in half. They would adze out a hollow in the flat side, and chop off that section, and then adze out another hollow, and chop that off. So the trenchers was a sort of rough oblong chopping bowls, as you might say. They didn't hang them on the trees, but just propped them up level handy to the spouts.

When they got their trenchers made or their buckets tightened up and cleaned and distributed around by the trees, they could start tapping. The Indians used to cut a gash in the tree just as if they was making turpentine. Gramp had got a little beyond that; he used a tapping iron.

Tapping out the old-time way.

A tapping iron looks like a big gouge chisel, and it was used the same way. First you chopped a kerf diagonal through the bark with an axe, and took out the chip. Then you simply drove the tapping iron into the tree at a right angle. Finally you put in a steel spout. They've come back to metal spouts again now; the oldest and the newest spouts is metal, and the wood ones that you occasionally see come from the time in between.

The auger to bore a hole for tapping is newer too; the old-time blacksmiths couldn't make an auger,

BLACKSMITH.

where they could make a tapping iron. The big old three-quarter-inch augers with a wooden cross-handle go along with the wooden spouts. You will find a great many old trees around here that have been bored with an old T-handled three-quarter-inch auger. Now of course they only use a half or three-eighths bit, with the small metal spout.

The old steel spouts was made by the blacksmith out of worn-out scythe blades. The blacksmith would cut off the heavy rim on the back to make nails out of, and bend the thin part into spouts. That was just one sign of how precious metal was in Gramp's time. That was why the blacksmith was such a big man in the community.

Spouts from worn-out blades or staghorn sumac.

The steel spouts they drove into the cut made by the tapping iron. The wooden spouts was whittled out of staghorn sumac. I've made them myself. You take a piece that is about right for size, and whittle it around to fit a hole the size of your auger. You cut away half of the spout on top, and just left the end that went into the tree round. Then you run a hot iron through the pith, and burned out a hole for the sap to flow through.

The science of tapping a tree is something that not many people know. The only results you get

36

from tapping comes from the sap growth, the outer growth underneath the bark. You could bore a hole clear to the center of the tree, and you wouldn't get no more sap than if you just bored two inches under the bark. There is only two inches' depth of sapwood on a tree. You can bore as much deeper as you're a mind to, and all you will do is hurt the tree.

Getting into the sapwood.

The trees don't seem to be damaged any by tapping. Some of the old holes in a big tree will be ten inches under the bark. Wherever you bore it makes a kind of an elliptical dead place, and that spot always stays in the tree forever, and the hole doesn't fill up; it grows over, but it won't fill up. You cut any old maple, and you will find the holes, far underneath the bark.

In deciding where to tap a tree, you pick out a place that has new growth. It's very hard to tell without you study it, but if you look at the tree, there will be new cracks or openings in the bark. As the tree expands, the bark doesn't expand with it, but keeps splitting open; that is why they are shaggy. If you look around carefully, you will find where the new growth shows on the bark.

The next part of the science is to set your buckets on the side where there is the most limbs, or the biggest limbs. The sap goes to the limbs, so you always look up a tree as well as at the bark. You look for the new growth on the side where the limbs will draw the sap. The ideal is to get more or less on the southeasterly exposure, but you tap on any side if the new growth and the limbs is right. When you are hanging four or five buckets on one old tree, naturally you have to hang some on the back.

The best limbs draw most sap.

Once a tree has been tapped, you musn't tap directly in line with the old tap-mark above it or below it. If you tap below it, you will get sap, but it's injurious to the tree. If you tap above it you won't get any sap. Just move out of line to one side, and it won't matter. The height doesn't matter in itself; you just want a convenient level for handling the buckets.

Well, you tap your trees, and you hang your buckets. Then you come back to the weather and the season, the same as Gramp done every day of his life. They've got their evaporators and their central-reservoir gathering systems and their state grading nowadays, but the weather is still the only thing that will make the sap run. Some years spring comes off warm early, and then you can't hardly buy a gallon of syrup anywhere in the area.

Freezing nights and thawing days to make it run.

To get a good run of sap, it should freeze hard at night and thaw daytimes. For a good sap day there must be a west wind and bright sunshine; it is very unusual that sap will run on a south wind.

The cold sap is the best quality; when there's an icicle or a trace of an icicle on the spout, you know you've got it.

When the snow goes and the frost gets out of the ground, the minute the buds begin to swell on the tree, the syrup starts to take on a leathery taste. It's like the difference between Scotch and straight whis-

key. What little sap runs after that is called the bud run; that sugar is generally just sold for tobacco sweetening.

If you do it right you can go on tapping the same trees long beyond a lifetime. The first job I ever had working out was in 1911 or '12, working for Ed Adams in Marlboro, and we tapped some pretty big old trees. I asked him how old he supposed those trees was. He said, "Well, I've lived here over seventy years, and when I was just big enough to carry a stack of six empty buckets, they seemed just as big as they are now." Those trees was really old growth, three and a half to four feet in diameter.

Trees are individuals, like cows. One tree will run a lot of sap, and another one only a little; one tree will run very sweet sap, and the next one will taste just like water. If you go around your sugarbush as long as Gramp done, you know all the trees individually. In the big lots some of them even had names. Up at Ed Adams's in Marlboro we used to have the Old Seeds, which was some big ones in a certain section of the sugar woods. That was one trip with the gathering tub. The next trip was on the west side of the hill; they didn't run much. Then you went down to Grandpa Moon. He was a tree about six foot in diameter, and went up pretty near to the sky, and never ran much. The next trip was to the Sprouts; they was trees probably a foot or more in diameter. Some of them Mr. Adams could remember when he mowed in there; the very youngest was about forty years old.

Sap differs from tree to tree.

The quality of the sap varies from year to year, too. Some years it's good, and some years it's quite sandy. And some years it's sweeter than other years, so you get more syrup for the same amount of sap.

It varies by year.

On an ordinary small farm like Gramp's, you would

39

generally set from two to four hundred buckets, which in a fairly good year might give you between twenty-five and fifty gallons of syrup. The year I worked for Ed Adams he set twenty-five hundred buckets, which is a big lot, enough for three or four people to take care of. We had a good season, with a run of around three or four weeks, and we made a ton of sugar. Mr. Adams had a gold medal award for sugar he'd put in the World's Fair, I think the Columbian one in Chicago, where he said people said that wasn't no sugar, it was soap, it was so white.

Four weeks is a long season, and it can go sour.

In a bad year the sap won't hardly run at all, to do you any good; in a very good year it may run as long as four weeks. It isn't usually steady. It will run a day or two, and you'll have a freeze-up, and it will stop entirely. Then it will start again and run two or three days more. As long as it freezes at night you're all right; you don't get the buddy taste. During some of these extra runs, the sap may even run all night, and the buckets will be full again in the morning. Then the buckets may start to sour, and intead of drawing sap away you have to draw water to the buckets, and wash them.

Gathering twice a day.

Generally you expect to go around and collect in the morning, and again in the afternoon. Nowadays they use a big gathering tub on a sledge, or even run the sap straight from the trees down metal gutters or plastic tubing to a reservoir. In Gramp's time you just lugged the buckets in by hand, and they got pretty heavy along toward night, specially if the snow was deep. The modern buckets hold around fourteen to fifteen quarts. The old ones was a lot more awkward, but they had two of the staves on opposite sides prolonged at the top, with a stick running between them for a handle.

A lot of people in Gramp's time used wooden sap

40

yokes, pieces of wood hollowed out to fit over your shoulders, with a semi-circle cut out for the neck, and a piece sticking out from the shoulder at each end. You would take two of your wide-bottomed wooden buckets, and hang them by cords on the ends of the yoke, and go to a tree. You would collect from one tree to another until your two buckets was full, or if the ones on the tree was full, you would just swap buckets and go back. In those days you wouldn't pretend to gather a great ways off.

Sometimes you see a sap yoke made of two bows fastened together at the ends, with two straps across in between for your shoulders, but I think those mostly come from Canada.

Before the time of the gathering tub, they would just go around and collect the sap, come back and pour it in a big kettle over a fire of maple chunks, and leave it to boil while they went back for more sap. When things got more permanent, they used what they called a sap pan, just an ordinary big iron pan maybe eight feet long and two or three feet wide. That's all I ever knew of Gramp's using. After that come the evaporator. There's different kinds of evaporators, but the idea is about the same in all of them. The Bellows Falls evaporator, for example, was a sap pan with crossways partitions. Each partition connects at one end with the wall of the pan, and at the other end it doesn't. The openings

Gramp's way of boiling was crude, then partitioned pans came in to make it an art.

41

are at alternate ends, so that the cold sap flows in over the fire on the front end, and zigzags through these partitions until it gets to the back end, which has a partition with a gate. You lift up the gate, and fill the back end. You shut the gate, and start watching your thermometer; the back end boils slowly because it's so far away from the fire, and when you get to the temperature of syrup or sugar—the sugar temperature is higher, of course—you draw the liquid off through a felt strainer into your cans or tubs or whatever you're putting it up in.

Sap beer.   In the old days they used to make a barrel of sap beer. They boiled it down a while to give it more pep; then they let it ferment, just the same as you make cider. I never knew of Grandpa's making sap beer, which may be why I never cared much for it. I don't think it's a very appetizing drink myself, but if you go back into the hills around Wardsboro at the right time you will still get some sap beer in case you want to try it.

Gramp's syrup was a black molasses, of course, but like I said, he would boil it on down to sugar, and pour it into crocks or tubs. He made wooden sugar tubs specially, and he would pour the liquid sugar right in, and let it harden in the tub. When they wanted some sugar, they'd just go in there and crack some out. Sometimes they might melt it. If they wanted it fine, they would pound it up. Ordinarily they used it in lumps just as they pounded it out for cooking, or in their tea. They didn't drink coffee much in those days, anyway. For sweetening they put it on the stove and heated it, because when it was melted you could measure it. They melted it for pancakes, too.

Tub sugar.

Sugaring-off is a big occasion around here. The young folks will come in for a party, with doughnuts and coffee and sour pickles. They bring in tubs of snow. They boil the syrup down until it will wax— a little past what the cookbook calls the soft-ball stage—and then they pour it on the snow. It cools right away into sheets or strips, not particularly sticky, and you can pick it straight off the snow with a fork, and eat it. The pickles cut the sweetness so you can eat more sugar.

Parties for sugaring-off.

In the old days they used to sugar-off sometimes on the kitchen stove, and they would hang a piece of fat salt pork from the stove shelf. When the syrup got to boiling up, it would hit that salt pork, and would flatten right out.

Once I knew of a man up in Marlboro that came there to live from Long Island or somewhere. They was having a sugar party up to the church. He went, and he got his dish of snow, and was going to have some sugar on snow. They poured the sugar on; he got to watching everybody, and took his fork, and started in. Then he begun to laugh.

He said, "I'm glad I didn't miss this after all. I came up here to find out what sugar on snow would be like. If it was white sugar, I had an idea it must be pretty thin eating."

43

After white sugar got to be common, maple sugar was something special and was mostly sold as cake sugar. The year I worked for Ed Adams, I think they sold a five-pound box of cake sugar for a dollar. That box would probably cost you around seven dollars now, if you could find it. I helped put the cakes up in nice clean white basswood boxes, with pinked paper. I remember they set me to pinking the paper with a toothed iron.

Why it got
to be a luxury.

When I was in Indiana I met a girl at Huntington who had what she called maple sugar and pecan nuts, a kind of black stuff. I told her she didn't know what maple sugar was, and when I was working for Mr. Adams I sent her out a box of the best maple sugar I could find. She wouldn't give in, though; she said that was maple candy.

Late years they think they have to have stirred sugar—a fairly recent invention. You cook it to the temperature marked for soft-sugar stage on your thermometer, and while it's cooling you beat it with a wooden paddle. It's like warm butter, and never hardens; it grains, but the grains are very fine from being beaten, and that makes it white. It makes a pretty good spread or a frosting, but it don't taste much like maple to me.

Maple cream.

Another thing they do in making these little candy hearts and leaves and shapes like that, they dip them in hot syrup while they're fresh. That glazes them, and keeps the inside from ever hardening.

In talking about sugar, I find I've done just like the old fox-trappers back in the woods. You would hire one of them to teach you how to trap foxes, and he'd tell you everything real careful, all the details that would catch the fox, only he'd leave out the one point, such as not touching the trap with your bare hands and leaving your scent on it. I've told enough

44

so that you would know better than the city people I heard of over in Whitingham, that was going to go into sugaring on a big scale and do it right. They bought all the best equipment, fancy evaporator and everything, and they was going to get their money's worth—said they wouldn't just play at it like the farmers up here, they was going to do it all year round.

I warned you about that. But there's one thing I left out. Some of my neighbors here don't quite find out about it until they're as much as seven years old. I do know of one prominent local citizen that was told, when he was about big enough to toddle, that he could have one tree to make his own syrup. He picked a beauty, too, a great big one right near the house, only he couldn't seem to get no sap, and finally he had to bring his grandfather out to see what the trouble was. Probably the boy was just absent-minded: the tree he picked was an ash.

It still starts with the tree.

His idea was about the same as a big outside concern I knew of that bought up a bankrupt sugar business somewhere in the northern part of the state. They was high-powered fellows that knew how to get up advertising would make your mouth water. They had the most beautiful colored labels and pictures fixed up that I ever saw. They was going to make a real going concern out of it.

They sure would have, too. But they must have got hold of some fellow like me that forgot to tell them everything, because judging from all these beautiful advertisements they calculated to get most of their syrup from hemlocks and ash trees, and not from sugar maples.

CHAPTER 4.

Doing with Stone

EVERYBODY KNOWS that Vermont is one of the stoniest places there is. In the long run even Gramp couldn't fight the stone, so he had to learn how to manage it.

The town of Guilford, where I live, had probably the oldest slate quarries in the United States. Government records state that slate was quarried in Guilford as early as 1812, but I've seen papers to show they was quarrying slate three years before that. Lots of houses around here have slate from cellar to roof. A house *Slate from* with a big cellar would have the bottom flagged with *cellar to roof.* square slate flagstones, instead of cement, which they didn't have. One place over in Vernon has a central chimney, with a brick room, like, in the cellar underneath, and inside the brickwork it is made up like

46

a cupboard, with slate shelves. Just up over the hill from me is a house with a flagged cellar, and the house itself rests on nice big pieces of dressed granite about six inches by twelve inches by maybe ten feet long. This same granite is used around here a good deal for posts.

Another kind of thick, slightly wavy slate goes for doorstones. My doorstep is one of those.

For doorsteps or siding.

The Estey Organ Works, which was started in Brattleboro in 1846, is slated all over, instead of clapboarded or shingled.

For maybe ten miles around Brattleboro you don't hardly ever see a swaybacked roof on a house, and that's because of the slate, too. If you figure a roof is going to have to carry slate, you frame it with stout timbers accordingly. Besides, Guilford slate lasts so long that the weather very seldom gets in to rot the ridgepole.

Actually the weight isn't the most important part, because quite often you get loads of wet snow that far exceed the weight of the slate roof, and on a slate roof the snow will slide off and relieve the pressure.

There is no roofing slate quarried in Guilford any more; nowadays it comes from over west, around Fair Haven, Vermont, and Granville, New York. Fair Haven slate is green or reddish, and quite thin. Guilford slate is dark gray, very thick and heavy.

Weight compared.

What killed the Guilford slate was the railroad. In Gramp's early days Guilford slate was shipped down the Connecticut by flatboat. Then the railroad come in and put the flatboats out of business; but rail rates were too high for carrying slate, and put an end to slate, too.

As a young fellow Gramp helped load slate from the Dummerston quarry on to the riverboats. One time the captain of the boat wanted to take back a full load down to Hartford. The slate was set up edgeways, and Gramp and the boys kept piling it in. Every time they asked the captain if he didn't have about a load, he said no, he wanted to fill her up.

They kept piling it on and piling it on until he decided that he had a load even if the boat wasn't full. He said, "All right, shove her off," so the boat crew started to push her away with poles. They give a big heave, and she went up at one end and down at the other, and took a little water, and then some more. She's down at the bottom of the river yet, so far as anybody knows.

Even without the Guilford quarries, Vermont still produces more slate than any state except Pennsylvania, which is a lot for the size of Vermont.

When the Guilford quarries was really going strong, about the time Gramp was born, there was as many as three hundred families engaged in quarrying slate just in Guilford. They were practically all Irish and Welsh. There don't seem to be anybody that knows how to cut slate today except a Welshman.

When Guilford had wars every Saturday night.

Every Saturday night there was always a war between Wales and Ireland. They had plenty of cider brandy in those days, and plenty of hard cider. It seemed to be a universal drink all around the country because they could get the apples and distill the cider easier than they could get whiskey. I imagine they liked to fight pretty well anyway, and the hard cider didn't discourage them none.

My house was a slate-digger's shanty, and right on my twenty-seven acres of land there's six quarries—I think. My big quarry is probably the next to the oldest in town. The oldest one is on the old Guilford road that goes over from Algiers village to Fort Dummer.

48

It's nothing to do with slate, but you might like to know why the east village of Guilford is called Algiers. Up until just a few years ago there was a couple of old ladies that still got very mad if they heard you call Guilford Algiers.

Algiers village gets its name.

Along about the time when the United States was having trouble with the pirates in the Mediterranean, Guilford and Brattleboro and Marlboro was all pretty much of a size, and there was some very hard characters used to live in those towns. It was John Gale that told me how the boys from Guilford went up and trimmed the Brattleboro crowd at poker, and then they took over the Marlboro crowd. Brattleboro and Marlboro got together and swore they was going to get even. So they had a great big bang-up poker game with all three towns in it, and Guilford cleaned them out again.

At that the boys from Brattleboro and Marlboro was just fit to be tied. They said, "You Guilford fellows are so crooked, you're nothing but a bunch of Algerine pirates!"

It so happens that Judge Royall Tyler, who wrote the first American comedy play, was living over to Guilford Center about that time, and wrote a novel that was very famous, called *The Algerine Captive;* but Algiers wasn't named after that, it was named after the cardsharps.

To get back to slate, five exceptionally large quarries were worked in my immediate neighborhood, and any quantity of small ones. Some was quarries for roofing and flagging slate. Then there's a slate that isn't building slate and it's not flagging, with a peculiar grain, which they call bastard slate. There is only one or two places where they quarried any amount of that; it made stone posts. One quarry is between my place and John Gale's.

Flagging or posts.

49

John Gale himself had a quarry for nothing but doorstones and bridges. The stones will come out, some of them, four and five feet wide, looking as though a stonecutter had finished the edges. You only have to cut the edge to make them square. The grain runs about four inches thick, and wavy, as I mentioned before.

The thickness of the grain has the most to do with deciding what kind of slate is in a quarry. The slate is always perpendicular in the hillside; it never lays flat. Slate is originally a mud formation; liquid mud comes up through fissures in the earth. The sides of the fissure squeeze together, and the lateral pressure turns the mud into slate.

How nature formed slate, and beginning the quarry.

In quarrying it they start on whichever side of the vein has the thin, roofing slate. These slate ledges always have seams; sometimes they're blind seams, so fine you can't see them with the naked eye, or sometimes open seams, but anyway there will be a rift so that the slate comes out all loose in big sections. They blast out a channel—in Gramp's time of course there was no dynamite, and they just used black powder. Then they begin splitting off the slate at the top edge. If it is too tough they will blast off a piece, but ordinarily they start with steel wedges and a small hammer. They put these wedges on a seam in the grain of the slate, and start a small crack.

50

Then they keep increasing the size of the wedges until they can get in a bar. Gramp would pry away with the bar, and as he bent the slab away from the ledge, he would drop a cobblestone in the crack to take up the slack. When the slab is bent far enough, it will break off in a large sheet, and fall over sideways. Generally there is a seam or shelf part way down the wall so that the slab will come loose.

The first slab.

They move the slab out where they can get at it, and start splitting off thin sheets. They do that with a thin steel wedge around eighteen inches long, which they drive in on the different grains.

To cut the thin sheets into roofing slate, Gramp used what he called a fence and a sax iron. The fence was nothing more than a thin iron bar with the ends bent down to form legs that was driven into a log. The sax was a dull, straight-edged knife, like a bolo, with a blade about a foot long, and a round wood handle not more than three inches long. On the back edge was a square punch, a sort of spur.

Gramp had a stick with inch notches in it, and a nail point for a mark. He would hitch the notch over the stones he split off, and move the nail to scratch off the size of the slate. He would lay the slate on the fence, and cut it straight along with the sax iron. After the slate was saxed out and squared up, he would turn it over and punch square holes with the punch on the back edge of the sax, the shape of the old cut nails they slated with in those days.

He sizes and punches the sheets for roofing.

Probably you don't see how a man could punch a hole in a piece of slate without breaking it into a hundred pieces. As a matter of fact, if you took a slate from off a roof and tried to punch it, it might shatter. But when the slate first comes from the quarry it's very easy to work—almost indestructible. It has what Gramp called quarry damp in it. You can

51

hold a slate up and strike it with a hammer; instead of shattering it, you will make a hole the size of the hammer-face clean through. Slate won't shatter until it has laid in the sun and cured out.

Guilford roofing slate was cut at random sizes and widths. They would make them as big as they could split off, the bigger the better. The largest ones was usually about three feet wide and two feet long. That sounds wrong, but I mean as it lays on the roof. Instead of making the slate reach up the roof the long way, they laid them wide.

As long as Guilford slate was being cut, they never used more machinery than a one-horse dumpcart. The drilling was all done by hand, and the blasting was with black powder; the splitting was done by hand, and the cutting was done by hand; the waste was wheeled out on a wheelbarrow. All these big holes around here was dug by hand.

Start big at the eaves, work up small to the ridge, and use every piece.

When it comes to laying a roof, Gramp would start down at the eaves with the longest slate he had, and lay it to a line. Guilford slate was too irregular-sized to go by the top edge, so he'd snap a chalk line across the course, and lay according to that. There would be one or two courses of long ones. Then there would be several courses one inch shorter, and after that more and more courses that got shorter as you went up toward the ridgepole. Gramp would lay a certain size of slate as far as he could go, and then cut them down an inch shorter. Maybe he started with slate two feet long at the eaves; at the ridge they would be seven or eight inches long and four or five inches wide. Gramp didn't waste none; he saved it all. Instead of a man buying all one size to put on his roof, like you do with asbestos shingles, he merely took enough to cover the roof. They figured out what it would take, and got out enough in ran-

52

dom sizes to do the job.

Sometimes the upper corners of the slate, the part under the overlap, was clipped so as to save weight, to make it lighter on the roof.

That old Guilford slate certainly is heavy. Once I was helping John Gale build a new house, and we was taking the slate off the old house, a hundred and fifty years old, to put on the new house. I had a man to carry the slate down for me as I took them off, and when I got to the ones at the eaves I give him one slate at a time.

Never too old.

Backing down the ladder he says, "What was these originally designed for?"

I said it was a slate, what did he think, and he said, "It looks like a tombstone to me."

Just then the lower rung of the ladder broke under the weight of him and that one slate, and I told him he'd better look out or it would be a tombstone after all.

After we got the slate off the old building, we put it back on the new one. An old Irishman that lived with slate all his life came to help us, and he said, "There is very few men that know how to flash a chimney, and I'm one of them." He done it, and it has never leaked to my knowledge. The secret is to use plenty of metal. You put the metal on the roof like a slate, and bend it in half up one side along the chimney about four or five inches. The mason puts a sheet of lead in the brickwork of the chimney, and the lead laps down over your metal. You lay the slate over the metal that's on the roof, and if you let the metal run far enough under the slate, six or seven inches, it will never leak.

The right way to flash a chimney.

If I was laying a roof new, I guess I'd rather lay Fair Haven slate, because it weighs about half as much; but the Guilford slate is almost permanent.

53

When they are good they seldom break and they seldom leak unless you have seconds or scraps. The slate on John Gale's old house had been on over eighty years, and he never had to have it repaired. I was fixing up a few broken ones on the back, and he said that was the first anything had even been done to it.

The bastard slate, which made posts, had to be split with a wedge and feathers. Feathers was little metal half-round wedges, like if you cut a dowel in half diagonal. The thin edge is turned back to make a little wing or hook. If you put two of them face to face, you can drop them into the round holes drilled along the line you're going to split, and the wings on top will catch, leaving a wedge-shaped opening between the feathers. What you done, you put small steel wedges between the feathers, and started tapping them lightly with a hammer. You went along the row tapping each wedge a little at a time until the stone split along the line of holes.

Drills, feathers, and wedges, plus a light hand and patience.

These holes was all drilled by one man using a short drill with a square shank at the top that tapers off to a round at the bottom. He held the drill in his hand, and kept turning it and striking it with a heavy hammer held in the other hand. It got pretty tiresome if you weren't used to it. The old fellows used to say you must catch the hammer on the rebound. When it bounds, keep on lifting it, don't wait till it stops. Then it wasn't hard work.

Most of the barposts around here have a wood piece bolted on that had the barholes cut in one way or another. Probably it was hard to work out barholes in that kind of stone; anyway I don't know of but one set of plain stone barposts around here, and they're just regular thick slate.

When I built the cow stable underneath my neigh-

54

bor Coombs's barn, I took out two stone posts that must have been between seven and eight foot long, about a foot wide, and six inches thick. They come out of the post quarry right on his property. One of those stones was just about all one horse wanted to snake out of there with a chain. They was originally for the barn to sit on, and they hadn't rotted any at all.

I don't know what slate and stone was worth in the old days, but not a great deal. The first time I repaired the old Slate Rock School in Guilford I looked up the old school district records of 1829, when it was built, and I found an item of twenty-five cents for a stone passover on the fireplace. The passover is the support across the opening; nowadays it's usually strap iron. Most of the old ones was slate, and sometimes you even found an oak timber. Those records said the building was to be twenty-four foot long and twenty wide, with a shed for the accommodation of the house—they meant the outhouse. Total cost, including furniture, was $171.50, and the land that it was on was leased for nine hundred ninety-nine years for five dollars.

Prices then and today.

Roofing slate was sold by the square, an area of a hundred square feet on the roof; it goes by the area laid to the weather, not the whole area of the squares themselves. Nowadays a square of Guilford slate would be around one hundred dollars—if you could find it—and Fair Haven slate comes to around sixty dollars.

Slate was cheap because what people prized then was the stone, not their time. I don't suppose Gramp ever really thought about his time being worth money; all he figured was whether he could get things done in time to keep up with the seasons.

Gramp was really more of a hand with the field-

Using fieldstone.

55

stones that worked up out of the ground. The land
hereabouts is strewed with these round, smooth stones
left by the ice sheets, supposedly. They are various
kinds, but mostly a granite formation that was
rolled in here.

When you start plowing a field regularly, and turn
the land in one direction all the time, you lose
topsoil to the depth of the plow each year at the
top of the hill. Plowing, along with ordinary wash
or erosion, keeps bringing up stones long after a field
has been cleared. And the first time they cleared a
field they would take out an awful lot of stones before
they could plow regularly.

Why rocks seem
to grow in fields.

They would plow once the best they could to free
the stones some. They would just dig out the small
ones with a spade. For the big ones they would
have to use the oxen and a stoneboat. They would
dig around them, and then flip a chain over the
stone with what they called a rolling hitch. It was
quite a trick to make the hitch stay on various different shapes of stone, because no two were alike. It
looked simple, but I can't even tell you what a roll-

ing hitch is like without I see the stone you're going to hitch on to.

Anyway, with a proper rolling hitch the oxen could pull the stone right out of the ground and on to the stoneboat.

A stoneboat is merely a large-planked toboggan, except the front end is not turned up so high. The planks was sawed special, nosed up at the end so that the front would run three inches or so from the ground. At the sawmill the planks was sawed straight to a certain point, and then put on the carriage at a diagonal and sawed the rest of the way so the nose turned up.

The stone walls both fenced in the fields and cleared them out. In preparation for the wall they would plow the loam where the wall was going, and shovel it out more or less to the subsoil. Then they would draw the stoneboat along beside this trench, and roll the big ones in for foundation stones. Quite often they would wall off a ten-acre lot, forty rods one way and forty rods the other. Sometimes it was only haphazard.

After Gramp had rolled the big stones off into the ditch, and set them to suit him, he would draw the boat beside of it. As fast as the boat come along he would take off the small stones that a man could pick up, and he'd place them right on the wall, and build it straight ahead just as easy as you please. He worked so fast you might have thought he was just throwing them in at random, yet when he got through, the wall was as solid as if it was one rock.

I can lay a dry wall of selected stones—flat ones picked out with the right size and shape—the same as I can lay up a well; I'll talk about that later. But I never could master the art of laying a fieldstone wall. Gramp done it for a lifetime, and I suppose I never

The stoneboat.

Dry walls begin with a ditch and the big ones.

Gramp's rule
for laying stone
walls that stand.

had a chance to get the practice. The instructions he give me for laying stone was to make each stone touch as many other stones as possible. A wall was double-faced—that is, it was straight up and down on each side, making practically two rows of stones. The stones must lean in so that they would bear against each other in the center, and the odd-shaped stones that wouldn't lay, what they called rubble, was filled in to complete the center.

If the wall was to be real fancy, and they had the stones to do with, the flat or semi-flat ones was put on top, and called capstones. They would go clear across the wall from side to side. Those walls will stay up much longer than the ordinary throwed-up wall. When they come down it's usually because somebody pulls them down to get the stone; digging up stone is too much trouble for people nowadays.

A man came along one day and wanted to buy some stones off from the wall along in front of John Gale's.

John told him he wasn't to take them off that wall. He said, "There's plenty of stone around here that you can have, but you can't have this. That wall still holds my cattle with very little attention, and my grandfather intended it should. He took pains to draw all those stones down from the hill a-purpose to build that wall, and that was a good hundred years ago."

"I don't blame you for that," the man said. "I guess I'll get my stone somewhere else."

When my helper on John Gale's roof talked about tombstones, he wasn't being so foolish as maybe he thought. I suppose you might call it the last use a man would ever have for slate; anyway, there's some beautiful tombstones made out of Guilford slate.

58

On the road from Algiers to Guilford Center, just opposite the Creamery Bridge (before you get to Brandy Bridge, which is named from the keg they used to encourage the workmen with when they was building the original wooden bridge), you'll find a high bank that's just covered thick with wild strawberries in the spring. There's a sort of scar going slantways up the bank, and that's what's left of the burial road to the Old North Cemetery in Guilford.

I go up there once in a while and look things over. There's a few Civil War veterans in the new part, over near the big maple, but I should guess there was more from the Revolution. Some of the oldest stones is like the ones you see in the old Boston burying grounds, with those jack-o'-lantern cherubs that have wings for ears, and "Here lyes" is spelled with a *y*.

I guess I must be kind of unreligious, like Gramp, because I pulled up some of the tombstones to set them straighter, and I found out stoneworking hasn't changed much. One stone, not the regular Guilford slate but more of a marble, was shaped kind of fancy on top, with a big semi-circle sticking out and two little ears, like. When I pulled it up I found the fellow had originally worked the other end, and something went wrong, so he just turned the stone around and started over.

But the ones I always notice more than any is nice clean Guilford slate, older than the fancy one but not weathered so much as the ones with the jack-o'-lanterns, and evidently all cut by the same fellow around 1815 or 1820. You can recognize his hand.

I know he was proud of his work for two reasons. One thing, when I pulled up some of his stones I found that down below the ground level he'd cut his guildmark. His stones had some real nice designs,

Stonecutting in an old cemetery.

59

and his lettering was good, but he couldn't spell worth a cent.

The other way I know for sure this fellow took pride in his art is that he wouldn't throw away a nice stone with borders and designs on it just for a few misspelled words. If he merely put the wrong letter in the deceased's name, for instance, he'd just carve a different letter above it.

When he struck a tough word like February, and carved it *Febary,* and decided that was wrong, he just put a caret mark after the *b,* and a nice neat *u* above the line, and he was satisfied.

I copied off one of this fellow's inscriptions:

> *The youth is gone*
> *His sole is fled*
> *His body is num*
> > *bered with the dead.*
> *His bounds is sot*
> *He can not pas*
> *There is not a sand left in his glas.*

CHAPTER 5.

The Animal Kingdom

GRAMP was never much of a hand for animals—didn't even get a great deal of time to go hunting. But all the same when I think back it strikes me as if the critters run him more than he run them.

You take the chores. Practically all the regular work that he done every day was on account of the livestock. The family just come in for an occasional thought.

The first thing was about four o'clock in the morning, when he galloped out to start the fire, fill the kettles with water, and see that the wood was in.

Up and doing before dawn.

Most generally the wood was brought in the night before with the kindling. That was about the last he would do for the family; then he was ready to go to the barn.

He would take the milk pail with him. The first thing in the barn was to feed all around. The old horse would have to have his, to keep his noise still, and then Gramp would feed the cows.

Feed the stock, milk the cows, take care of the milk, then sit down to a real country breakfast.

Next he would do his milking. Gramp was no dairy farmer; he just raised enough for his own use. There wasn't much of any real dairy farmers in his time, anyway. They couldn't ship large quantities long distances without refrigeration, for one thing. Anyhow, Gramp would bring in the new milk, and strain it into pans to set. Then he would take the temperature on the thermometer, and write in his diary what the temperature was and what the weather looked like. Those entries and a few accounts was about all he put in his diary.

By that time the rest of the family was supposed to be up and have breakfast going, and he would eat around half-past six or seven o'clock, probably.

Breakfast was generally cornmeal mush with cream; they didn't care too much about having it sweetened, but if it had to be sweet they used maple syrup. Other times it might be corn dodgers—that's cornmeal griddlecakes; they had tea, not coffee, and quite often doughnuts. The wheat flour for the doughnuts was a local product too; I can remember seeing the remains of a bolting machine, for cleaning the flour, at the Larkin mill in Centerville before it burned down.

Breakfast and dinner was likely to be the same in one point—for one or the other they'd have boiled potatoes and pork.

Then he would start on the day's work. If he was cutting wood he would go to the woods about eight, until ten or eleven o'clock. He would about get up there in time to come back for watering.

He used to water the stock once a day around noon. They didn't have none of these fancy drinking

fountains that a cow can learn to work with her nose; they turned the critters loose to make their own way to the brook. Sometimes that was quite a distance.

While the stock was gone, Gramp would clean the stables and put the feed in the mangers. He always cut a small popple stick two or three inches in diameter, and put that in the horse's manger. When the horse had the bark all gnawed off, and part of the stick maybe eaten up, Gramp would put in another one. He said the poplar bitters was good for him.

The young stock wasn't turned out until after the milch cows was back in, because the young ones stayed out all afternoon. In cold weather they could run under the sheep shed. Hereabouts the old sheep shed invariably faces to the east, and your barn breaks the wind from the north, so there is a sunny corner in the barnyard. Gramp would throw out dried corn fodder, generally, and let them chew on that and play around as long as they were a mind to. They came in when he done the evening chores.

He would have dinner around noon, after he watered and fed. If he hadn't had meat and potatoes

Back by mid-day to clean, feed, water, and let the young ones out to play.

for breakfast, he'd have them for dinner—ham, or fresh pork if it was winter, or occasionally beef. According to the season he might have boiled dinner (corned or salt beef, depending). And for breakfast and dinner they ate an awful lot of pie. In winter it would be apple, usually; in the wild-berry season it was berry pie; in early spring it was rhubarb. Most everything can be made into pie. Mince was a favorite; Grandmother would make up the mincemeat and save it in crocks, covered with a coating of fat or tallow so that it would keep.

After dinner Gramp would go back to the woods, or wherever he was working.

At four o'clock in winter it begun to get dark, so he would come back, tie up the young stock, feed all around, and get down the hay for morning. Then he would have his supper—Gramp never ate anything but johnnycake and milk at night—and after he had sat around long enough to get rested, he would go out and do his milking, and set his milk again. When he got in the wood he would be done for the night.

He would generally get in the wood around supper if he could find a moment; he would split his kindling and fill the woodbox. If he could find any fat pine splinters, he used them for kindling; otherwise he just took corncobs and any dried popple stick or dry pine and stored them in an old milk pan. Paper wasn't very plentiful. He always used his knife to start the fire; he'd take a splinter, and whittle down shavings, leaving them on. He shaved down round and round until he had an accumulation of shavings around the stick that he could light with an eight-day match.

In his boyhood days, before they had matches, he had to go borrow some fire from a neighbor if theirs went out. He told me his way was to take a little

piece of bark, and put some ashes in it, and then a few live coals in the ashes.

Sometimes the neighbors' fire would go out, and they'd send their boy up to Gramp's. This boy would just scoop up ashes in his bare hand to carry the coals. Gramp said he never figured out just how the boy got home without dropping the fire, but somehow he always made it.

Of course they always churned their own butter, in a Bennington churn. Those was quite common around here; outside of a museum I have never seen anything except a Bennington churn. The wood dasher-churns went out around here way, way back, even before Grandpa's time.

Churning cream through "swell, break, and gather" in the tall Bennington crock.

The Bennington churn is a tall crock with a pottery cover. The dasher is a round stick with a flat wooden cross nailed through the center to the lower end of the stick. The cream was poured into the crock, and when they was ready to make butter they merely took the cover off, and replaced it with a wooden cover that had a hole in the middle for the dasher. Pottery covers with a hole was used for churning too, but they mostly got broken, and Grandmother had a wooden cover.

They churned right in the crock, working the dasher up and down. In making butter there is three stages to the cream. In the first stage it starts to froth

65

like whipped cream, and it swells, so the crock mustn't be too full before you start. After the cream swells it starts to break—that is, it turns into kind of a floating curdly mess. Then after it breaks it will gather. The three stages are the swell, the breaking, and the gathering. When it gathers, it gathers into lumps: first little granular ones, and then a single big lump.

When it had gathered slightly, Grandmother would pour the buttermilk out, and put in water; she finished gathering it in cold water. That way the butter was practically washed. She never had a butterworker other than a big tray with two paddles. She would take these two paddles, and work the salt in and the buttermilk and water out. She would take a pat on one paddle, and square it up with the other.

I don't believe Grandmother was quite so fussy as Gramp about how things looked, apart from having them good; otherwise she would have used a butter stamp with some design to make a fancy-looking pat. Those wooden stamps was the predecessors of the square pound prints. To use them, you soak the mold first in boiling hot water, and then in cold water; that way the butter won't stick to it.

The difference between getting het up, and giving up.

Talking of butter, you remember that old story about the two frogs that fell into a pail of milk, and one of them give up and drowned, and the other kept on kicking until in the morning they found him floating on a pat of butter. That was one of Gramp's favorite stories. It was one of his great hobbies never to give up, even if sometimes he did get excited and throw things. He was always telling me, "Never say die."

Gramp was a musical soul, and a great one for singing. He used to sit and sing to the cow while he was milking. He told me once he set down to milk and begun to sing a Civil War tune: "In my prison cell I sit, thinking mother dear of you," and just when he got to, "And the fiercest charge we made," the old cow hauled off and kicked him. All he said was, "I didn't tell *you* to charge." After that I guess he sung less warlike songs while he was milking the old cow.

When the cattle went out to pasture, around the second week in May, the dry or young stock was

generally put in one pasture, and left there all season. Times when Gramp didn't have two pastures, the stock would all run together, and he would just bring in the milch cows. Quite often he would milk them and turn them right back into the pasture. Going after the milch cows was always a boy's work; I used to prod Grandpa's old cow home once in a while.

He put the cattle out to pasture from May until snow time.

He would usually bring the cattle in by the first of November, according to how the grass was. Some years they got snow by the first of November, and there wasn't much of any feed, so that was about the time he calculated to take the stock in.

Gramp saved manure all winter. When he cleaned the barn he would pass the manure out the windows of the stables. The windows had sliding board doors over them, to save glass, I guess, and so's they wouldn't get broken. Anyway Gramp would slide the windows open, and pitch the manure out with a fork. That's why you saw the manure pile right next to the barn, where it rotted the sills.

Spreading manure from the dumpcart was part of the spring work. The cart was tipped part way,

He spread manure
by hand rather
than put salt and
sand on his land.

chained and blocked so it wouldn't dump or level off. Gramp always made five piles out of a load, about ten big steps apart. He would hook the stuff down off the cart with a manure hook that had a very strong old hand-shaved handle about two inches thick and six feet long; it had four broad tines, hooked downward.

The actual spreading was done when he started to plow. He would go down one row of heaps, spreading with a fork, and go back and plow it under.

Manure for the potato patch was generally drawn out some time in the fall or early spring. It had to be shoveled over two or three times to leach it out, or you would get scabby potatoes. The potatoes was manured in the hill; you plowed a furrow, and put the manure in the furrow.

Grandpa never believed in commercial fertilizer; he said phosphate was nothing but salt anyway. One time he put some in water, and poured the water off to see what he got in the bottom, and all he had was some sea sand. The fact is that they used to use sand as a body to put the chemicals on, where now they use phosphate rock—crushed limestone that is supposed to contain superphosphate. Anyway, Gramp wasn't going to buy no crushed rock when he could have all the manure he wanted.

Gramp always had a few hens, but he wasn't a poultry-raiser, no more than he was a dairyman. When the hens laid, they just simply hatched chickens, and some more grew up. There wasn't any special breed; I guess they was what you would call All American, all kinds and colors. Any rooster that had queer markings, he was kept for future breeding.

If they wanted eggs, they would go out and hunt around to see if they could find some. Gramp never bothered with henhouses. If he knew where there was

a nest, he went to that until the hens started to set, and then he'd have to find another one. The hens just lived around the place on scraps and whatever they happened to pick up. Once in a while Grandmother threw them some dried corn on the cob.

Of course foxes and skunks would get some of the chickens and eggs, but not enough to be missed very badly.

People usually think the woods in a new country must be all full of wild animals. I suppose they are,  more or less, but some of the wild animals thrive much better where the land has been cultivated and then grown up again. In Gramp's time there was practically no deer in southern Vermont. The first ones was brought in by the state from over in New York, and released with tags in their ears. I never knew of any deer until I got to be fourteen or fifteen years old, and there wasn't but four or five days a year when you could shoot them. Now they're a regular pest in Windham County.

In Gramp's day it was mostly small animals—woodchucks, hedgehogs, foxes, skunks. Foxes was just

something they hunted for sport; they weren't worth anything. The hedgehogs was kind of a nuisance sometimes; they'll eat the helve off an axe if you leave it outdoors overnight.

To Gramp, woodchucks was the most useful game, because he could tan up their hides. By the time he taught me to trap them, steel traps had come in, and snares was against the law; in his younger days he made snares with a thin sapling and a cord.

Woodchucks are caught in warm weather, so Gramp would take the hide off, fill it full of salt to keep the flies out, and tack it on the barn or the back of the shop to dry. When he had accumulated two or three, or wanted some rawhide, he would get out a box of wood ashes. He would take out most of the ashes, lay in the skin, cover it over with ashes, and wet it; then he would put in another skin, another layer of ashes, wet that, and so on.

Every day or so he would go around and try the hair, to see if it stuck or if it would pluck. When he thought it was just right, he would take them out and scrape the hair all off. After that he had to wash the lye out of them. He would rub them between his hands before he hung them up to dry, and if they didn't feel just right he would have to wash them again, sometimes three or four times. Then he had to taw them to get the stiffness out. What he did, he drew them back and forth over the edge of a board; this made them limber. When he got through they were a nice creamy-colored rawhide, fit for flail thongs or snowshoes or anything like that.

Tawing and a dido turned woodchuck hide into whips and snowshoes.

People used to wonder how he got rawhide of any length out of a small chuck skin. What he done was perfectly simple: he cut what they called a dido. He just went round and round, and cut a spiral as long as he wanted. The thickest skin was on the back, so if he needed a real strong thong, he'd cut from there. The hide on the belly was thinner.

The longest and strongest thongs went into braided whiplashes (or sometimes plain thong lashes if they was stout enough), and into snowshoes. Gramp had a pair of homemade snowshoes that he laced himself, made of ash and woodchuck rawhide, with some hair left on. The hide was varnished. He didn't do much hunting by that time, so it was only just for some necessary trip off into the woods that he would get out his snowshoes, and plug along, and turn around and look behind sometimes to see how he was doing. It was pretty tough going. Myself, I never learned to walk on snowshoes until I was grown up, and then I wished I hadn't tried it.

I said a while back that the most prized thong for a flail was an eelskin. Before there was so many dams in the Connecticut, there used to be a lot of eels in the brooks and rivers around here; they would run in schools up all these streams. You could see them going up through in the daytime. And the greatest fishing was going after eels, because you could go nights when you wasn't doing anything else. Gramp and I used to bob for eels with a float. You let the float lay on the water with the hooks down in the

Going after eels.

71

bottom; we used just ordinary worms for bait. With a lantern we could sit there and watch, and when the float begun to bob, we knew we had a bite.

Birds weren't too plentiful; there was no pheasants, and just a few partridges. Gramp used to tell me about hunting wild pigeons sometimes. In his day great flocks of these passenger pigeons used to fly north, and in the fall they'd go south again, which made two or three days of pigeon-shooting. But as near as I could find out, about the only way you could ever catch them was while they was asleep.

By my time of course Gramp had got rid of most of his livestock; before that he kept the same animals as anyone else—a pig, some sheep, and his oxen.

He always calculated to raise a pig, and feed it soft corn. Soft corn was corn that didn't cure down hard, and wouldn't make good grain.

They would kill the pig around Christmas. Lots of barns still have a round log wedged in horizontal up high inside the door, to hang the carcass from. Gramp always smoked his own hams with cobs and hickory chips, or sometimes apple chips. He smoked them in a barrel. He set his barrel in the side of a bank, and dug a small flue inward and up the slope to the bottom of the barrel. The pan of cobs had to set in the flue leading to the barrel, because when the heat went up in there it made the fat pieces of meat drip, and if they dripped straight down on the pan of cobs, the whole thing would blaze up.

The ham hung by thongs from a stick across the top of the barrel. Gramp kept it covered, and kept the smudge going underneath. In three days the ham was smoked; then it was hung away in a dry, cool place in the back pantry.

Sheep in the old days was one of the most important things a family had. Every farmer had about

72

thirty sheep, which kept him in light, clothes, mutton, and partly in soap. All these old farms around Vermont have an open shed with a pen on one end, generally facing east or southerly, hitched on to the barn. The posts in the open front was set on two cobblestones, one on top of the other, for the same reason that they put two stones for the hub of a zigzag rail fence—to keep the moisture from crawling up.

Old-time farmers kept more sheep than cows.

Gramp would shear the sheep in the spring before turning-out time, along about the last of April. They

sheared with regular shears, like garden shears, in those days; now they have electric clippers. After the ewes had had their lambs was the time for them to shed for the summer, and that was when the shearing was done.

The wool was the principal thing; that was how Gramp got his clothes when he was a boy. If he needed a new pair of pants, they had to shear a sheep; his mother carded the wool, and spun it on a wool wheel. Wool wheels are larger than flax wheels—something to do with the speed that the fibers are drawn out at. They run the big wheel with a hook or dolly that they kicked the spokes along with, or

Mostly for wool.

they might just use their hand. I don't think his mother wove the cloth; that was done on a neighbor's loom, and then she made up the clothes afterward.

The everyday buttons were wood disks with a scrap of cloth left over from the making of the garment. Great-Grandma simply gathered the cloth scrap over the disk, leaving the top smooth and a small lump on the bottom; she sewed the lump on the bottom to the garment, and there you had it, button and coat matching perfectly. She done all the knitting, too, of course.

Anything that was to be dyed, they generally boiled the yarn with butternut bark, which made a sort of gray-green color. They used indigo some, but that was commercial coloring, quite expensive, and very little used. I've read that in those early days butternut-dyed homespun was the mark of a plain farmer and common citizen all over the country.

Dyeing yarn with butternut, and dipping tallow candles were just routine when Gramp was young.

Another important thing was the tallow for candles. They took the leaf, or any other fat part of the sheep, and put it on the stove where it was warm. That was called trying out the tallow—they practically cooked it until the tallow was melted nearly all out. Then they would put it in a bag, and hang it up, or somebody might hold it up. They took a lard squeezer, which was just two boards maybe three inches wide by two and a half feet long, hinged at one end with a piece of leather. City people are always finding them in the attic when they buy a country house, and wondering what they are. To use a lard squeezer you simply pinched the bag between the boards and squeezed the ends together, and the rest of the hot grease came out, and only the tissue was left.

Once the tallow was squeezed out, they could go to work and make candles. Gramp made tallow dips up to the time when the tin peddlers come around and

74

begun selling candle molds. To Gramp, a candle mold was a modern labor-saving device.

To make tallow dips, he would take pieces of a regular candle wick, called a tow, and loop them over a series of sticks. Whittling candlesticks was something you done to keep your hands busy on winter evenings. Gramp would dip a series of tows on sticks into a pan of melted tallow, then hang them up and let them drip. As fast as they cooled, he re-dipped them. The tallow was just barely melted; if he had heated it hot, it would all have run off, and he wouldn't have gained nothing. This way the dips gradually got fatter, and when they was large enough to suit him, he just clipped the loops that was doubled over the stick, and there was his tallow dips, ready to use.

With a candle mold, all you had to do was hang the tows down in, and pour the mold full of tallow, and let it harden.

Not so much of the soap was made from mutton fat or hog fat. The mutton fat went into tallow, and the hog fat into lard. But beef fat and refuse fat wasn't so good to eat, so it went into soap.

Gramp would take beef fat and old bones and anything else that might contain grease, and boil it up in a big soap kettle. As the grease came to the top he would skim it off with a brass skimmer. Sometimes if they had nothing better they would use a wooden paddle.

When he had collected the grease, he would start leaching the ashes. For that he used a wooden tub that had no bottom; it set on a plank with a channel cut around the tub, and a groove cut on the lower side to let the liquid drain out. He would fill this tub full of wood ashes, and keep pouring water on it. When the water soaked down through the ashes,

Making soft soap.

and drained out at the bottom, it was lye water. He added that to the fat, and soft soap was the result.

I spoke about oxen. Of course they done all the work that tractors do now. I don't know as Gramp would have agreed with me, but I guess I like the motor age better.

I never tried to drive oxen but once—just to take a load of hay into the barn. I done everything just right as far as I know. I walked on the left, and carried the whip in my right hand. (If a man says he don't know you from Adam's off ox, he means the right-hand ox.) I had one of the regular old whips with a four-foot hickory whipstock an inch and a half thick at the butt, tapering to the outer end. The lash was braided rawhide with a couple of thongs on the end for a cracker. Those whips looked wicked, but Gramp was just touching their necks to direct them, the way you'd neck-rein a horse. If you whip an ox you'd get him unruly. Besides, oxen actually are temperamental; they can run, even if they do act kind of slow.

Anyway, I hollered, "Come here, haw," and drew the lash against the far side of the off ox's head, and the team turned toward me all right. They went a little too far, so I hollered, "Gee off," and snapped the whip to the off ox, and crowded against the near

There's also the saying about dumb as a driven ox.

ox. That got them straightened out all right, and we went along nicely until we got to the barn door. It was a door with two halves, and one was shut. I yelled "Whoa," and a couple of other things, and tried to crack the whip across their noses, but they didn't understand me, and they went right along in with the load of hay, barn door and all.

I made up my mind I couldn't drive oxen.

Gramp never was much on cats, but if you had

a barn of course you couldn't live without one or two. I remember an old cat that used to hang around in the shop, and where he would scrape up shavings to kindle the fire with, she was likely to make a mess. He didn't like her very well, and one morning when things wasn't going to suit him, he found she had spoiled some more shavings.

He says to me, "You take that cat up behind the barn and bash her head on a rock."

I was about a dozen or fifteen years old, and he was pretty loud and positive, so I thought I'd better do it as long as he said so. I didn't like the job very well, but I didn't know what to do.

Up behind the barn I took the cat by the hind legs to swing it over my head, and she hooked her front claws into my back. I pulled a little, and she pulled a little, and finally I let go.

I went down to the shop, feeling real guilty and miserable, and he asked me if I killed the cat.

I said, "Oh, yes," and he said, "Well, she just come down here with her head in her mouth." The cat got there before I did. Gramp wasn't mad any more, and that was the end of that. I don't suppose if he'd have had to do it himself he would have gone in the first place.

Another thing, he never kept a dog himself. With only around thirty sheep to a flock, you didn't need sheep dogs like what they have in the old country. In fact Grandpa didn't like dogs very well. I know one of our neighbors had a dog that was pretty apt to nip anybody if they came around the place, and so when he went over there he took two small sticks, one in each hand.

I asked him what for, and he said, "I'll show you if that old hound comes out."

The old hound come out all right, and Gramp made as though to hit him with one stick; the dog watched that stick, and Gramp hit him with the other one. They kept that up until the old dog got sick of it and beat it.

You can see from this that Gramp was never a drover. Of course it's a dead letter now, but as far as I know the drovers' law still exists in Vermont: cattle, sheep, turkeys, and geese may be driven on the public roads as long as they're attended. In Gramp's time the drovers was always traveling up and down country in the fall, taking their livestock to market.

Naturally a dog was a pretty important assistant to a drover, and there was one well-known old character who used to go down to Hartford from where he lived, somewhere up in the middle of Vermont, and make arrangements with all the tavernkeepers on the way down to look out for his dog. He'd stay in Hartford for a spell, and send the dog home by himself. The dog just went from tavern to tavern, being looked after by the tavernkeepers, until he got on home by himself.

The innkeepers and the drover's assistant.

Back around the Revolution, John Gale's family used to run the Liberty Pole Tavern on the spot where his house stands now, and that was how John come to tell me about the drover's traveling dog.

In the winter, anyone that couldn't take a long winter without a little excitement would go traveling by sled, carrying frozen bean porridge to eat on the way; all the tavernkeeper could get out of them was a little something for stabling the animals and lodging the man. These trips had to pay for themselves with some profit, so people would take along miscellaneous loads of what they had to spare for trading. Quite often several neighbors would make up a load together with things like cheese, shakes, flax, cider vinegar, furs, or hides—anything they could trade in the city for needles, pins, rope, powder (not face but gun), and bar lead for bullets. They also brought back bronze buttons for dress-up clothes. The most important thing of all that they brought back on these trips was the much-prized English tools and English steel. All these winter sprees was generally to Boston, which they really did call the Hub in those days, and meant it.

Trading to Boston was their winter spree; in summer it was boating downriver to Hartford.

In summer most of the trading was done in Hartford, by way of the boats on the river.

Another time John Gale told me about an old fellow that was a great cut-up, down to Algiers, and he got so obstreperous that they appointed John to be his guardian. John had just got made a lawyer, and was twenty-one years old, and this old fellow was about seventy. He always called John "father," and asked his advice real solemn, but he hardly ever took it.

One time he got to cutting up so much that they shipped him to Newfane, to the county jail. Newfane jail was a great place for the prisoners, because one end of the building was the jail, and the other end was a hotel, and the prisoners got the same food as the guests. I've heard people say the guests wasn't as well pleased as the prisoners.

Anyway, they finally let the old cut-up out, and he had to walk back almost twenty miles from Newfane to Algiers. It was a good enough walk for a man of seventy, and along about dusk, somewhere in the neighborhood of West Dummerston, he heard a rooster crow. He allowed as how that rooster was simply asking for a little excitement, so he sneaked over and pinched him.

A little farther along the road he heard another rooster, so he went in and left the one he had in exchange.

Along about Brattleboro he done it again.

He said he made a good trade each time, and he always wondered which was most surprised, the farmers in Dummerston and Brattleboro, or the hens.

CHAPTER 6.

From the Woods

I GUESS I SAID BEFORE that almost anything special Gramp wanted, he just went out in the woods and looked up at the trees until he found a straight one of the right kind. He'd cut it down, and usually before the day was over he'd have what he wanted.

A lot of the time it was more important to have a tall straight tree than to have any particular kind, but choosing the wood was important too. For instance, you can't build a log cabin out of hemlock with the bark on, or it'll rot in a couple of seasons.

Gramp's special wood for implements or anything to be durable was white oak. White oak grows in this section, but not west of the Green Mountains very much. We have black oak, red oak, and white oak.

White oak for lasting strength.

The most wonderful thing to me that Grandpa ever made was a door from the house into the shed; it had wood hinges and a wooden latch, all of white oak. The hinges was two brackets on the door casing, with a round pin carved on the top of each bracket. The ends of the cleats that held the boards of the door together stuck out beyond the edge, and they were bored to slip down over the pins on the brackets. The latch was a small white-oak board too, with a string that went through; the latch rested in a wooden catch. In Gramp's day that was the only kind of lock most houses had: you pulled in the latchstring, and there was no way of opening the door from outside. That was the origin of the saying that the latchstring is always out to your friends. It meant they could always get in.

He used it in his masterpiece.

Another thing that he often made out of oak was sap buckets. Modern pine sap buckets can be stacked one inside another, but Gramp's couldn't, because the bucket was small at the top and large at the bottom. The reason for that was because it was so much easier to spring the bottom in. He would cut the staves in a uniform width out of oak, and then he would bevel the edges so that the staves would make a circle. He had a pattern figured out beforehand to tell him how many staves he needed; the beveling was done mostly by fit-and-try. Finally he planed them to make a tight fit.

The hoops was all wood too. He would split off a spline—maybe of hickory—and shave it to its proper size. He would bend it, and cut the two ends in a sort of hook shape, so that one would lock into the other.

Generally staves and hoops both had to be soaked in hot water for a considerable time; he would leave them kicking around in the hot water until he got ready to use them. Now and then he would try them to see if they was limber enough to bend.

When he had his hoops ready, he would put on the top hoop to hold the staves together; he would just press the bottom right into place in the groove he had cut around the inside of the staves, and then he would drive the hoops down, and pinch the bottom in tight.

Buckets for sap or for water were usually oak, with hickory hoops, and not one bit of metal in any of them.

Water buckets was made like sap buckets except the sides went straight up and down; instead of having a bail for a handle, two staves on opposite sides was longer at the top, and a stick run between them for a handle. One thing about those old buckets, they hung higher, and a small boy could carry one without dragging it on the ground. But they were good and heavy, all the same.

I told you about the little boy that tried to get maple syrup out of an ash tree. As a matter of fact you can't even get much of any syrup from most kinds of maple. The sugar maple, or rock maple, is the only one that anybody with sense would tap. Red maple and white maple will both give sap, but it's very dark, and the sap isn't sweet at all, so nobody taps them. They go mainly for firewood.

Striped maple is what the boys call whistlewood—

a little tree never much beyond the size of a shrub. It has very smooth bright green bark with white stripes. It's not used for anything except whistles—the bark slips easy, like willow bark.

Gray birch is just a small weed tree. Black birch, yellow birch, and white birch are good lumber trees. White birch was fairly useful for things that didn't have to last indefinitely. I'll tell you later about the birchbark canoes the Indians sometimes made. Gramp never made much out of birch except chopping trays and brooms. He made the chopping trays the same way he done with the trenchers for sap-gathering: he would split a good white birch log in half, and then take the adze and strike in from the ends. After he had dug out the center, he would turn the whole thing over, shape the ends, hew the outside a little, and shave it smooth.

There was two kinds of birch brooms that Grandpa used to make. To make a shaved broom he would take a white birch probably two inches or more in diameter. He might tie cornhusks around the end for a guide as to how much to shave back. He would start at the bottom and shave up toward the handle end as far as the cornhusk marker, round and round, till he had made enough splints to satisfy him. That would leave a core at the lower end, and he would cut it out from among the splinters. Then he would turn the broom around, and start up on the handle, and shave toward the other splints. Of course he wouldn't go far enough to let the upper splints come so close to the lower set that they'd split off. Then he would turn down the second lot of splints—turn them inside out, you might say—and bind them around with braided cornhusks or any other withes he had handy. He would work the handle down slim to suit himself.

Shaving a white birch sapling in to a broom was a spare-time chore.

84

A shaved broom was supposed to be dipped in water every time before you used it, to keep the splints pliable and prolong the life of the broom. If you do that, they last a long time, and they are just as nice as any broom you ever used.

Birch-twig brooms was easier to make, and had to be renewed oftener. Gramp would shape a birch handle, leaving a bulge like a cone on the lower end. This handle would go on from one broom to another. He would take a bunch of brush—any kind of tough twigs, but usually birch because they grow more long and slender—and cram it into a small iron hoop. He would drive the handle, top first, up through the middle of the bunch, and of course the bundle could never come off, because of the bulge at the lower end of the handle. When the twigs gave out you just knocked the handle out, and put in some more twigs.

Ash was another wood that Gramp used quite a lot. Rake handles (stales, he called them) and pitchfork handles was nearly always ash. He used it for most levers and handles where he needed a strong wood.

Black ash or swamp ash was what he used to make baskets. Grandpa was a great hand for baskets—small ones to pick apples in, two-bushels that were all you could drag around, cheese baskets with a two-inch octagonal mesh like a big chair seat, and grain baskets.

First he would take the bark off a small ash, and then soak the log. When he thought it was well softened, he would take a big wooden maul made up like a potato masher, or in later years an iron sledge, and just whale the stuffing out of the log. You've noticed the growth rings in logs. There's a soft ring and a hard ring each year. The soft ring of ash gets spongy when it has soaked; then you can pound the

Ash is good for pitchfork or rake handles, and makes stout baskets that take a hard beating.

Black ash for the
body, white ash
for the rim,
maybe oak in the
handle—and never
a nail.

log, and the hard layer can be stripped off lengthways.
That was the way Gramp got the long splines to weave
his baskets. If the basket was to be fancy, he had
to lay the splines on a bench and smooth them off
with a plane. Ordinarily he left them right in the
rough, and the basket would be a crude-looking work.

He started the bottom like a mat, with the splines
sticking out like the spokes of a wheel. Then he wove
in the filler, round and round, until he had the
bottom as big as he wanted it. Next he put it on a
round chopping block and bent down the splines
that stuck out, to make the shape of the basket. Then
he went on weaving the filler in and out until the
basket was full size. Modern baskets are nailed around
the rim, but Gramp wasn't going to waste no valuable
nails. The body of the basket was black ash; the edge
he bound with a strip of white ash. The handles was
bent out of white ash, or occasionally white oak, with
a notch cut to make a sort of fishhook on each end.
He would drive the handles down through the bind-
ing, and the hooks would catch on the filler, and never
pull out. Gramp's baskets would all stand a lot of
use and hard beating. They were rounder on the
bottom than the commercial-made baskets we have
now. With his pattern he could make them very near
to an exact bushel, though naturally not United
States standard.

Axles were a
science in ash.

Ash made wooden cart axles, too. The first one I
saw made, I complained that it wasn't straight, and
Gramp give me a lecture on cart axles. The wooden
axles where the hub turns are more or less cone
shaped; on the old oxcart there was a ring on the outside, a washer to hold the wheel on, with a pin. If
Gramp didn't have lard oil to grease the axles, he
would use any rancid grease or fats that wasn't fit for
soap.

When Gramp made the axle, instead of running the ends straight out he kind of cambered them a little toward the lower front corners. He told me that to have the cart run right, the wheels should dish under and toe in. If they run straight, the neap or tongue that the oxen drew the cart by would swing back and forth, and almost knock them off their feet.

Being a wheelwright was an art all to itself, but Gramp got pretty good at it. His wheelbarrow was a masterpiece.

He made a wheel with four spokes. The hub was square to start with. Then he worked that into an octagon. After he had centered the ends, and put in his iron pins for axles, he took the drawshave and rounded the ends of the hub so that it started from a square to an octagon down to a round. The wheel was about two feet high, with an iron tire that he got put on at the blacksmith shop.

His wheelbarrow had an iron tire and two iron pins.

The sides was cut out of a crooked plank that had a special curve in it. Starting from the wheel it curved down, then came back and up slightly, and finally the handles dropped down again, so that when you picked the wheelbarrow up by the handles it pitched forward and rolled right along on the wheel.

It always seemed to me about the size of a one-horse dumpcart.

Beech was a rather coarse, strong wood that went for hard work, like the body of wooden planes, or anything that took a lot of scrubbing, such as a threshold. Any place where there was friction, you would find beech. They used it for levers and for ring-dog handles. A ring dog is used to roll big, heavy logs; it is a ring maybe six inches in diameter with an arm ending in a sharp hook, pivoted so that it will swing parallel to any pole that you stick through the ring. They slide a pole through the ring, and the arm hangs down with the hook pointing forward. They drive the hook into the under part of a big log, and the butt of the pole rests on the top of the log. They heave up on the pole, sometimes two or three men at a time, and the hook rolls the log away from them.

A cant hook, which you will find around most Vermont farms, works the same way only the arm is hinged straight to the handle, and there is no ring. The handle is shorter and the hook is usually smaller than with a ring dog, and you can't roll such big logs.

Gramp's method of logging was the same one they have come back to now. They use tractors, and he used oxen, but that's about the only difference. He would cut a tree down, limb it off, and bob the whole tree—draw it out without cutting it up. He would cut it up into lengths as he wanted it afterward. It was only when they begun using horses that they would cut the tree up into twelve-foot lengths on the spot, and use a scow or a scoot. Gramp and his oxen would just drag the logs on the ground.

With horses, specially if they were drawing firewood, they would use a dray—wood-shod in the old days; now they're iron- or steel-shod. A dray is a

88

short sled with a body pivoted on a pin, practically the same as a traverse sled with the back sled knocked out; it has the poles dragging out at the back. Drays was used in rough places, and generally loaded crossways with four-foot wood. A team of horses will draw more on a dray than on a sled, and it's much safer because it won't tip over so easy, and the horses don't get hurt so often. But as I say, a tractor is more like an ox, and they've gone back to the old ways.

Drays for horses.

Elm had just one main use: for spike-toothed A harrows. The thing about elm was that you could generally find a symmetrical elm crotch with both limbs pretty near of a size, and spreading evenly. Gramp would leave a sharp tongue, like the blade of a wishbone, at the front to hitch on to, and hew the whole fork smooth. Then he would put in a crosspiece part way back between the limbs. When he put the crosspiece in, that made the A. Then he would bore holes down the limbs and along the crosspiece, and drive in his iron harrow teeth, whatever he could find. He would bore a hole through the front tongue, and put on a clevy, an iron bent in a U shape with holes in the ends for a crosspin. He would hitch the oxen on by the clevy, and then he was all

Elm went in A harrows, to use among stumps.

ready to drive around and harrow among the stumps.

Slow-dried elm
for his ox yokes.

Elm also went into ox yokes. The timber was either hewed or sawed at the mill, and then taken home and buried in the haymow. Gramp would simply leave it there until he got ready to make his ox yoke. If he happened to want to make one when the barn was full of hay, he was out of luck; he had to wait until the hay was down to where he could uncover the sticks. The idea was that the hay would absorb the moisture slowly out of the elm, drying it gradually so that it wouldn't check. It was something like a kiln-dried stick.

Hickory to bend.

Hickory was a strong wood that would bend good. Most bent things was made of hickory with the bark on. Gramp would simply soak it, leaving the bark on the outside, and then bend it and fasten it in shape until it dried. He made rake bows that way, and he whittled rake teeth.

I told you before about chestnut, and how it was used for ties, fence rails, and sometimes for houses.

Paint brushes
of basswood bark.

Basswood he just used by chance if he found a straight stick growing along his path; he never looked for it special without he wanted the bark. If you shave off the outside of basswood, you find an inner bark that is quite thick, sometimes up to half an inch of layers of a seamy texture. You put that in hot water, and then pound it, and it will make a wonderful brush to spread glue or paint or pitch or anything you like. Gramp always made his brushes out of basswood bark. The inside bark can also be stripped out and twisted and woven; the Indians sometimes made cloth that way.

Gramp wasn't too fussy in his choice of the hard woods between beech and ash and hickory and white oak; I have seen things he made of one or the other, just whatever came handy at the time.

He never had much to do with soft wood; just once in a while he would hew a stick of pine because it happened to be straight and tapered right.

The one place he always used pine was for pump-logs. After they got tired of bringing water from the well a bucket at a time, they figured they'd pipe it from the spring; and the only running water they had in those days came through the wooden pump-logs.

These logs was pine logs about eight feet long, and anywhere from four to six inches thick. It took three men to bore a log, and I guess it was a kind of a bee to see what they could do. They had a log auger that bored a two-inch hole, with a big T handle probably three or four feet long. They would dog down the log on a bench so it couldn't move. They had a guide like a sawbuck to start the auger with. One man would stand on each side so as to turn the handle; the third man stood behind it and sighted the auger to make it go through the log straight. He took hold of the center, and held the auger rigid in the sawbuck guide, and at the same time steadied it to keep it from running crooked. The other two men, one man pulled down on the handle, and the other pushed up, and they yanked it round and round and round until they bored through. You could go through from either end, bore a hole part way, and

Hollowing young, straight pines to make water pipes.

then start from the other end to meet it; but they had to be good men to do that.

After the log was bored, they hewed it down somewhat with an axe, and then shaved one end down sort of pointed with what they called a hollow auger. It smoothed up the outside so that it would fit tight into the reamed-out end of the next log. Each log had a cone on one end and an inside cone on the other; it was a snug fit, and they didn't leak too much once they was buried. Even to this day I know where I can dig some up. As long as white pine is kept wet it will never deteriorate, even if it's a hundred years.

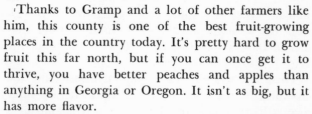

He chose white pine because it won't rot as long as it's wet.

Thanks to Gramp and a lot of other farmers like him, this county is one of the best fruit-growing places in the country today. It's pretty hard to grow fruit this far north, but if you can once get it to thrive, you have better peaches and apples than anything in Georgia or Oregon. It isn't as big, but it has more flavor.

When Gramp was young, the apples stood helter-skelter all over any old farm. A man would graft shoots on to the first thrifty-looking wild apple tree he found. They used to trade scions from one farm to another, and made a sort of hobby or pastime of it.

Gramp would gather the scions in late winter, generally around February; or sometimes he would cut them in late fall, and put them downcellar. Anyway, he would bury them up in moist earth in the cellar. The grafting begun in late March or April.

The scions was about two inches long, and probably as thick as a pencil, cut off at both ends. You cut them off by pressing them against the edge of a knife with your thumb, and rolling them back and forth.

To graft them on, Gramp would saw the top off the branch of a wild tree, and split what was left, the stock, down the center with a chisel or a knife or something. He would wedge the cleft open a very little. Then he would shape his scions on the bottom end, and very carefully insert two scions in each side of the cleft. The outside bark of the scion and the stock had to jibe exactly. Then he drew out the wedge he had put in to begin with; the cleft in the stock closed tight on the scions, and he was ready to wax.

Inserting scions in the stock.

Grafting wax was a mixture of beeswax, mutton tallow, rosin, and linseed oil. The idea of the mixture is that it musn't run in hot weather, nor crack off in cold weather. Gramp carried it out to the tree in a dish of warm water. To apply it, he would roll a piece of wax into a small ball, lay it on the end of the stock between the two scions, press it down, and work it around the base of the scions, making sure the entire top of the cut was covered. Then he would wax the crack down the side of the stock, and finally put a very tiny bit on the cut-off tip of the scion.

Waxing the graft.

Besides getting a thrifty tree to carry the scions, Gramp used to amuse himself by making one tree bear two or three varieties of fruit from different grafts. Mostly he grafted pears and apples, and occasionally some stone fruit. Generally, of course, you can only graft an apple scion on an apple tree, and so on; but it happens that you can make a pear grow on a thornbush, which Gramp would do sometimes for a joke. Cherries he mostly grafted on wild cherries; they were better trees than nursery stock, and would grow nearly as high as a church steeple.

Apples, cherries, pears, and jokes.

All grafting has to be done before the buds start to swell. That means you have to graft stone fruit— peaches, cherries, and plums—much earlier in the season than apples or pears, because the buds start sooner.

Nowadays fruit wood is considered pretty stylish for furniture and things like that. In Gramp's day apple was just firewood; occasionally you found a table or chest made of cherry; but the main place for cherry was in clockworks. Cherry is next to mahogany when you want a wood that stays constant, and doesn't shrink or swell with the weather. A wood clock won't keep as good time as a metal clock, but a cherry clock will keep better time than a maple one.

Cherry instead of brass for clocks.

Lots of people that have wood clocks think they must be very ancient because they come from a time when people didn't know how to make metal clockworks. Of course really it was the other way around: they made brass works first, but brass was scarce, and they couldn't turn out cogwheels in big lots. Then some whittling Yankee fellow in Connecticut, I understand, figured out how to machine them out of cherry by the hundreds. The wooden works was just a newfangled cheap substitute for metal.

CHAPTER 7

Grandpa's Tools

I'VE HEARD of hired men that was always refusing to do whatever was asked of them, and saying they could do it all right if they just had the tools. Gramp made it a point not to be like that; Gramp had tools for everything. His shop hitched on to the wood-shed of his house in Vernon; it was a small building something like twenty by twenty-four, but it was a regular museum. He had mostly wood-framed tools that he made all himself, except for the iron parts that he'd have to get from the blacksmith.

To give you an example, whenever he went out in the woods looking for a tree to make something special, he would give me three axes to carry. He always had an axe for each operation on the tree. His cutting-down axe had a handle a special length to fit Gramp's own particular size. The scoring axe had a

Out in the woods with three axes.

long handle. The broadaxe, for hewing after he had scored, had a shorter, offset handle, and was hung right-handed. Broadaxes have a blade twelve or fourteen inches long, and the eye—the hole where the handle fits in—goes at a slight angle. The point of that is that when you strike the axe into a log, the handle must swing out to one side or the other, depending on whether you are right- or left-handed, enough so that your knuckles will clear the log.

Once Gramp had found a tree to suit him, he would take the first axe from me, and chop it down. Next he would take a chalkline, a hard string rubbed with chalk. It used to be my job to hold it down at one end. He would hold it tight, and then snap it; generally it would snap out of my fingers the first two or three times because he pulled so tight. Snapping the line would make a long, straight mark of chalk dust on the tree.

The first for felling, the next to give something to bite on, and the third one for hewing right to the line.

Next he would take the long-handled scoring axe, and score along down the line. That was to give the broadaxe something to bite on when he begun squaring a timber. He would take the broadaxe, and come down on the scored line at an angle that would take a thin slab off the side of the log, the same as you do at a sawmill. He would strike hard enough to carry the axe just about through; with a little up and down motion of the axe he would take off the slab down the log. You've heard about hewing to the line; this is what it was. It took a pretty good man to hew right to the line every time, and not strike off to one side. Gramp would hew to the line every time; I never seen him miss.

Another thing about hewing with a broadaxe, the blade must go absolutely straight down. Everyone has a tendency to cut under. If you do that on each side of the log, the timber will be wedge shaped. So a good man like Gramp always strikes straight down.

After he had hewed two sides, he would cut the limbs off the tree enough so that he could turn it over and hew the other two sides; up until then the limbs was what held the log steady for him. Gramp could square a timber in a surprisingly short time— not but a few minutes. A good man could do it fast enough to compete with a sawmill in some circumstances.

Hewing ties for the railroad was quite an industry in the town of Vernon. There was no sawed ties in those days; there was beginning to be a few portable mills that would saw ties, but a hewed tie was worth about twenty percent more than a sawed tie. Of course it took at least twenty percent more labor, too, but the railroad people preferred it. There wouldn't be so many rejects because of poor-quality wood, and so you always had a sale for hewed ties.

Why the railroad paid more for hand-hewed ties.

Besides the three axes I had to carry for him, he had one that he called a cutting-up axe, for cutting cordwood with. The handles was all different lengths, all made by himself, out of hickory. Many years before I was born he had worked out the exact lengths of helves (the right name for an axe handle) that suited him, and when he got one just right he would draw a pattern of it, and cut a piece of board the proper shape and size, to be kept in the shop permanently.

Generally the hickory stick for the helve begun as a quarter split out of a log. He would take this quarter, and hew it into a square or stick of timber with his hand axe on a chopping block in the shop.

Squared sticks begin his helves.

The hand axe was very much the same as a small broadaxe, only with a handle not much over a foot and a half long.

When he got his stick hewed to a square, he'd lay

the board pattern on it and draw around the pattern, marking the outline of his helve. He would hew around that so he had a rough contour of his helve. He would put that on his shaving horse, and go at it with a drawshave.

The shaving horse was really a kind of vise—a four-legged bench, with a heavy plank hinged at the far end, and extending maybe halfway toward the seat end. The seat end was what you straddled when you was using the horse. The upper plank had a stick pivoted a little way from the free end, which went down through a slot in the bench. The top of the stick was hooked over to form a clamp for the work; at the bottom was a crossbar to put your feet on; there was a series of holes in the middle that you put a pin through to adjust the clamp for the thickness of the work. Pushing with your feet clamps the work down tight. The harder you pull on your drawshave, the harder you push on your feet.

After he roughed out the helve on the shaving horse, he would finish it up nicely with his spokeshave. It was much shorter in the blade than a draw-

Then the pattern, and roughing it out on a horse with a drawshave.

98

shave, and curved; it had a wooden body, a steel blade, and a brass throat.

After the spokeshave, he took broken glass to finish off the helve. Sandpaper wasn't much in existence; if he wanted any, he had to make it by gluing sand on to paper or cloth with glue made from horns and hoofs. About every old farm had a heavy iron pot of horn glue, and it was a sweet-smelling thing when they got it going. It was a small iron pot that they set inside of another iron kettle. Anyway, with all that trouble and smell, Gramp preferred to use pieces of glass to scrape down axe helves, rake stales, flail staves, and woodenware.

Grinding the axes was almost as much of a science as getting the right helve. For instance, a splitting axe to split wood with was ground very blunt. Not dull—Grandpa always wanted his axes sharp—but they was ground down thick just back of the cutting edge, what was always called the bit, to make them split the wood better. The other axes was ground thin, as you might say, but they also had to be ground so that the sides humped up a little. If you ground them straight like a wedge, when you struck into a stick there would be resistance as far as you went in; but if the head was rounded out, there would only be friction at one point, and besides the thickness would split the wood apart.

The broadaxe was only ground on one side, like a chisel. If it was ground on both sides it wouldn't have traveled straight, so Gramp ground the outside, and left the side toward the log flat. He hung his axe with the helve offset opposite the flat side to protect his hand. In grinding an axe you must roll it on the stone, instead of holding it steady.

All the grinding was done according to Gramp's eye, and I can tell you it had to be just about so. He

Grinding each axe for its different job, so one was fat, another thin, or like a chisel; but all of them had to be rolled.

99

supplied the brain and I done the work, or at least it seemed so when I was small. His grindstone turned with a crank; he didn't have it fitted up with a pedal so that he could turn it for himself. There was a little wooden bucket (or in my time one of the little oak barrels that white paint always came in) hanging on a tripod over the grindstone, with a little hole in the side and a straw to drip water on the stone.

Taking care of his grindstone.

Then he had one stone with a trough underneath. The trough was kept full of water; it could be dropped down when it wasn't in use. Gramp said you musn't never leave the stone in the water—that softened it. And it mustn't be left out in the weather, because that softened one side. If the stone had to be left out in the weather it should have a board or something over the top, or else the soft side would make the stone get out of round after you ground with it a little.

Chisels was something Grandpa ground entirely different from the axes. Gramp had a sort of jig to hold his chisels steady; the same for planer blades. The jig was a flat piece of board with a roller on the bottom. He would hold this roller on the grindstone, with the chisel laying flat on the board and reaching down over the roller. He had a little adjustment—

Steel chisels were precious, and got special treatment.

I'm sorry I can't tell you now just how it worked—so he could change the angle for different blades he had to grind.

After Gramp had ground a blade on his grindstone, he might hone it on a piece of Norway Crag oilstone, some sort of petrified wood, if he wanted a real fine razor edge.

The chisels Gramp had were cast steel, and naturally very precious; even the blacksmith didn't make them. Grandpa didn't have such a large collection as he would have nowadays.

There was the framing chisels, very heavy, with a thick blade. Take a narrow one, and the blade would be twice as thick as it was wide. The framing chisel was two inches wide, because all tenons and mortises are two inches wide.

The way they done that, if they wanted to use a timber for framing, they would mark the mortise two inches wide and generally about four inches long. Then they would take a two-inch auger, and bore two holes through each two-by-four-inch oblong pattern. After that, all they had to do was to drive the two-inch chisel down in, and it would square the holes up.

This is as good a place as any to tell how they framed houses in Gramp's time. I wouldn't bother, except that sometimes people used to the kind of wood houses they build now, with two-by-four studding and some plywood slapped on for siding, don't know what a framed building is. They think frame means it is a wood house. What it is, it's the stoutest kind of skeleton—mostly eight-by-eights—the members joined with mortises and tenons, and pinned with trunnels. Just hitch a tractor to a corner of one of these buildings, and try to pull it over: you can't do it. At the same time, if a cornerpost rots and the building starts to lean, you can right it by jacking up the corner and pulling the whole thing back in shape. And it's as good as it ever was.

There is hardly anyone knows how to frame a building any more. The houses in Gramp's day was built all on the ground. The fellows that was doing the carpentering hewed out the timbers, bored the holes for the pins, shaped the tenons, and cut the mortises. They knew their work, and did it well, but they didn't split hairs over measurements. In

Real framed houses built the old way have heavy timbers and oak-pinned joints, and they are a far cry from the flimsy things slapped together today.

101

fact when Gramp was whittling the white-oak pins—treenails, called trunnels—they had to be a little bit off, and fit tight, or they wouldn't hold. Gramp originally whittled out or split out the pins by hand, but later on he made a steel ring that he could just drive a pin through, and that would shape it as near as he wanted.

Treenails wanted to be a bit off.

When the building was ready to put up, they had a raising. Everybody would attend from all around, and they had refreshments, a big dinner, and generally a barrel to help yourself to. Of course the women all had to come to help get dinner for the men.

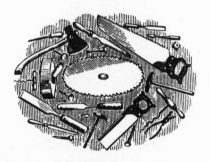

The parts that the carpenters had got ready was all put together on the ground; at the raising they connected everything together, and lifted it up.

In the morning everyone wanted to work up high, and drive the pins on the high timbers. Come night they preferred to stay on the ground; the barrel of Jamaica rum, or it might be cider, looked a lot better than the rafters. I went to a raising once, and I guess there was fifty people there, but there wasn't more than five or six that was ever doing anything. Those five or six were really working, and knew what they were about, and the rest of them were just there to the raising, doing the heavy looking-on, same as I was.

It helped to make a raising high.

There have been three different bridges at what they call Brandy Bridge on the way over to Guilford Center. When they built one of the bridges, the selectmen worked on it; they had some brandy to help lift the stones with, and they drew one of the selectmen home on the stoneboat.

Another reason besides the shortage of iron why they pinned the frames was, they used great big timbers that you couldn't hold with any spike I ever see. The rafters was quite often just small logs hewed on one side to lay against the roofboards, and some of those ridgepoles would be twelve-by-twelves thirty or forty foot long. Gramp used a mallet to drive the pins, because it didn't mull the pins up so bad, and he wasn't so apt to split them as with a hammer.

By the time they got one of those roofs framed up with twenty-four-foot rafters, and a purlin running lengthways under the center of the rafters, and the purlin in turn well supported, they had a pretty stout structure.

Twenty-four-foot logs for framing a roof.

I had a little experience with one roof framed that way, with log rafters, and shingled. It was a barn. The wind blowed the big doors in, and blowed the

103

whole roof right up off from the plate, so it flapped up and down in the breeze like wash on a line. The pins pulled out of the plate, let the roof drop, the rafter slid down over the plate, and left the ridge-pole so that it sagged down in the middle the whole length. And there's a big barn down the road in Massachusetts where the hay fermented and blowed the whole roof right off into the next pasture. I guess freak things like these make an argument for slate roofs instead of shingles. The weight of the slate would have held the roof down, and done justice to the framing.

Getting back to Gramp's tools, I almost believe he had more different planes than what he had chisels. They was all made with a wood block, generally beech, for a body; he used to make his own. The blades was held in with little wooden shims or wedges; putting the blade into the plane was a very fussy operation.

Gramp's planes ranged from the unhandy jointer for truing edges, to a block pitched shallow to cut across the grain.

The blade had a different pitch according to the different work it was used for. The three principal planes were the jointer, the smoothing plane or jack plane, and the block plane. The block plane had a shallower pitch than the others, because it was used to cut across the grain.

The jointer was a long plane, a great old wooden block about two feet long, with a blade something like two inches wide. Once or twice it slipped off the board and fell on my feet, and I can tell you I remembered it; it was awful heavy. I got quite spry dodging the jointer. The jointer got that name from being used to level off the joint between two boards set side by side, but mostly Gramp used his to true up the edge of a board, and make sure there was no hollows or bumps on the edge. The plane was so long that the

104

blade would skip the hollows and catch on the high spots. You had to keep running the plane until you could take off a shaving all the way from one end of the board to the other.

The smoothing plane was shorter, maybe eight or ten inches long, not so unhandy as the jointer. It was just used to finish up any rough surface.

The block plane, the one with the shallow-pitched blade, was for easing up the end of a stick that fitted too tight, or for any kind of shaving ends across the grain.

Another thing you don't see any more, now that they have sash factories, is wood-molding planes. Gramp didn't go in too much for them, but he had a plane for making window sash, with a shaped blade, and a groover (a very narrow blade, adjustable so that you could plane off a channel and leave an edge standing on each side), and a wooden rabbet plane that he used to make shiplap with.

He had fancy planes to mold a sash, and one for rabbeting weathertight shiplap.

Shiplap was what came before the modern tongue-and-groove matchboarding; Gramp used it when he wanted something that was going to be real weathertight. When he and I boarded up the north side of the shop, we shiplapped it to keep the wind from blowing through. For shiplap you cut away half of each long edge of the board, like a step. Then the next board will lap over it by the depth of the cut.

Then Gramp had a various number of saws. I think he sort of collected them; ordinarily if a man had two saws he was pretty well off. Gramp's ran from the bucksaw, which was really about the most important, down to little pointed compass saws. He used to make those out of an old caseknife or anything like that—file the teeth out for himself. He had to buy the files to do it, but even the files had the teeth cut by hand. They would heat a piece of a flat, carbon-

105

steel bar, and put it in a toothed jig, and then a man would move the tool along, and strike in the teeth by hand—of course only on one side. Then it was cut to length.

The old saws was every bit as good as modern ones when it come to doing their work. I've got an old bucksaw around here now; I sawed up most of my wood with it last year. It cuts fast—it's even fun to cut wood with. It has been used so much that the blade is wide on the ends and thin in the middle.

I don't know whether Gramp made all his own saw grips, but he made his own bucksaw frame. Instead of the steel wire tightener you see now, he used a rawhide thong with a stick twisted in the middle. Of course you must never leave a bucksaw tightened up; they're generally left in the shed, next thing to out in the open, and a change in weather might snap your blade or crack the frame. So when he wanted to saw wood, Gramp would twirl the stick around between the thongs until the blade was taut, and then catch the stick crossways over the middle bar of the frame. When he was through, he would slack off a couple of turns.

The same kind of files that Gramp used when he made his own compass saws, he would use to sharpen the saws that got dull. You probably know that in

Never leave a bucksaw tightened.

106

order to cut good a saw has to be sharpened with a file, and then set—the points of the alternate teeth have to be pushed out sideways in opposite directions. Setting saw teeth. If the teeth aren't set wide enough, they don't make a wide enough cut, and the wood you have already sawed through pinches together on the saw blade. Nowadays saws are set with a special kind of fancy pliers called a pinch-set; Gramp used a hammer-set— an iron with a beveled edge. He would lay the saw on this iron, and strike the first tooth with a hammer, then the third, and so on, skipping every other tooth. Then he turned the saw over, and went down again. With a small saw he used some kind of punch, but the old-fashioned two-man crosscut saw was big enough so that he could just use a small hammer and hit each tooth direct.

Another cutting tool that Gramp had around was a shingle frow. He didn't use it much, because there was so much slate for roofing. It was a big, awkward- looking, thick sort of knife blade with a socket at one end to hold an upright handle about eighteen inches long set at a right angle to the blade. You set the blade into the end of a cedar block, and drove it down through with a maul. The shingles was split off the block one at a time—shakes, they called the hand-split ones.

Splitting shakes.

I talked about the various augers, like for framing and for sugaring. In his early days, when he had to depend entirely on the blacksmith, Gramp used a pod auger instead of an auger bit, because even if the blacksmith was a great man, he didn't know how to make a spiral bit. The pod auger was shaped about like a long, pointed fingernail, and it worked the same as if you dug your fingernail into a bar of soap and started turning it. Gramp used a wooden brace to turn the pod auger.

Pods instead of spiral bits.

107

Iron shovels are something else that's new since Gramp's boyhood. He had to do all his digging with a wood shovel made in one piece from a straight piece of wood. It had a D handle, and the only metal part was an iron shoe on the foredge of the blade. The blacksmith used to hammer out the shoes; they were sort of folded in two lengthways, giving you a groove you could slide the blade in to; then the free edges was nailed down.

The virtue of a wooden shovel.

These wood shovels would do for a ditch or anything you would use a square shovel for now; they are still best for snow. I don't think they would have been so good for postholes, but then Gramp never dug postholes. He used to drive posts with a big wooden maul.

Forks had to be made by a blacksmith, and I imagine they was mighty valuable property.

I said before that Gramp used to scrape things down with glass. Anything that was real fine he would polish with pumice, and oil it with boiled linseed oil to give it a shine. He used to finish things like chair rounds that way, after he had got a fairly true cylinder. His way of doing that he copied from the Indian method of scraping arrow shafts down with broken flint or broken chips of quartz. The Indians would have a stone with a hole in it, sometimes soapstone and sometimes slate; they would scrape the arrow shaft until it would just go through the hole, and that would make it uniform. Grandpa's way was to bore a hole in a piece of stick for a gauge. He would shave his chair round or handle or whatever it was by eye with a spokeshave, and then he would start scraping with glass until the work fitted the round hole. He would scrape off parts that bound in the hole, and finally he would have a fairly smooth, even round.

He followed the Indian way of shaping rounds.

108

Horn things he just made by eye. He had one horn that he used to keep trinkets in, and one for matches, with the point cut off and a wooden bottom fitted in. Of course he had powder horns, like everyone else, and then if he helped butcher any cattle and a horn struck his fancy on account of the shape or the variegated color, he would ask for it.

Modern carpenters have a lot more and more accurate measuring tools than Gramp did. About the main one he used was a wooden level that also acted as a straightedge. It was a long board, with a center line carefully scratched at right angles across the side from one edge to the other. Then there was a square hole cut across this line, standing on its point, you might say, so that the center line ran diagonal from one corner of the hole to the other. There was a string attached to one edge of the board at the center mark; it served as a plumb line. With the hole, you could see whether the string was hanging just at a right angle; if it was, your board was level.

His level was a board, a hole, and a string to act as a plumb line.

Gramp used this kind of level in laying walls and in framing houses. Of course it wasn't as accurate as a spirit level, but then Gramp's work was mostly on hewed timbers, not cabinetwork at all. He used to say if you got it within a quarter of an inch that was pretty close.

The first time I remember going in to Gramp's shop, I discovered that each saw hung on a peg, and each axe, chisel, or plane had a place that looked as if it was probably made for it. If I'd been old enough to think about how people behave, of course I'd have known that Gramp would be bound to keep his shop like that. I found out pretty soon anyhow, because about ten minutes later Gramp begun showing me

In his shop.

109

how to use a cutting-off saw. He showed me how to place my thumb on the grip, and my forefinger straight ahead to steer the saw. Then he told me always to let the saw do the work; all I had to do was run it. If it wouldn't cut, it needed filing, but I mustn't never ride on any saw. The saw done the work, and I was merely the operator.

After I had kind of taken that in, and got my arm a little tired, I started to hang up the cutting-off saw (they call them crosscuts at the hardware store) on the nearest peg in the wall. Gramp looked around, and there was a roar that you could hear practically over in Guilford. I had gone and put the cutting-off saw on the split-saw peg.

That was the first lesson I learned about carpentering; the next one, and the one I remember best, was

how to use a hammer. Gramp said the average boy or girl or unskilled carpenter would take hold of a hammer quite close to the head, and he told me to take hold out on the hammer handle, or else saw it off. He made me reach out on the end of the handle to get a good swing; that would give the nail a heavy blow.

Every time I got up close to the head, he would say I was pushing the nails in, not driving them.

He used to teach me all the time; anything that he was doing, I worked right along. If he was building a chicken coop, nailing cleats on to some boards for a door, I would put my cleat on my end of the boards, and he would put his on his end. Then he would criticize the one I put on. If it was crooked, I would have to take it off and put it on all over again. If I bent the nails over, I would have to take them all out, and pound them straight, and put them back in.

Rule of thumb.

Of course with a small boy holding a big hammer by the long end, I used to bang things up quite a good deal. Finally I said to Gramp, "How do you keep from pounding your thumb?"

He said, "Hold the hammer in both hands."

111

CHAPTER 8

What He Had to Buy

IF YOU'VE READ what went before, you know this is going to be a short chapter. When Gramp first went to farming, the blacksmith was about the only man that ever saw any of his money. As he got older he begun to buy more things, until by the time I come along he was practically as bad as a city fellow —or anyway he thought so.

Quite a few little industries did grow up for a while in the local villages. John Gale told me there had always been a mill or some sort of shop on the site where the Algiers general store is, ever since the town started. There was a blacksmith and wheelwright shop. There was a baby-carriage shop. There was always a gristmill until just a couple of years ago.

A few gristmills still keep running in Vermont;

Village mills and shops.

there was one just closed down up to Putney. Now-adays they mostly grind cornmeal for city people who get it by the pound; naturally there isn't much grain raised around here any more. The mills grind a little feed too, but nothing to what they did.

There was a horn-comb factory in Algiers. Even when I was a boy, all combs was made of horn. They boiled the horn to soften it, flattened it out, and then cut combs from it. They also made horn buttons at that shop.

Linseed oil, to shine things up with, was another thing Gramp had to buy. There used to be considerable flax raised around these parts, and I said before that people made their own linen. But the oil had to come from an oil mill, and there was one here in Guilford. One of the stones is up in a dooryard just off the main road.

Down on Broad Brook at the falls, a few hundred yards below the general store, there was one of the old vertical sawmills. John Gale used to have the old up-and-down saw from that mill in his shop. If Gramp wanted timbers for framing, of course he hewed them out himself; but planks and floorboards and such as that had to be either got out in a saw pit, with one man on top and another in the pit, or sawed out at a mill. The up-and-down mill was just one step beyond the saw pit; the water would turn a wheel that worked a long, thin saw (like a huge bucksaw blade) up and down. The log rested on a bed that run along by a ratchet. Every time the saw went up or down the ratchet kicked the log along. They must have changed the speed of the ratchet according to the thickness of the log. The up-and-down mills sawed so slow that the lumbermen used to say if they wanted to saw a big log they would put it on and start the mill, and go home to dinner. Pretty soon

Planks from the up-and-down saw.

113

after they came back from dinner they could start the next cut on the same log.

The Guilford statistics tell how many sawmills there was in town, and there wasn't any that had a capacity of more than 1500 board feet a day, except one that could saw 2000. The average little portable mill now, with a power-driven circular saw, will run about 6000 to 8000 board feet a day, up to 10,000 if they're pushed.

If you look in most books about the New England pioneers, you will read where the first settlers cut down all the trees and burned them for ashes. The Needham side of my family—my father, his father, his father, and his father—all burned wood to make potash for soap; that was their business, selling potash, and had been ever since the State of Vermont started. They begun in 1794, and kept it up for three generations. But actually the fellows that wrote the histories got all excited for nothing.

The settlers had more sense than they often get credit for.

Good timber was just as valuable then as it is now, and the old-timers had better sense than to destroy it. What the first settlers burned was of no value. It was old growth, either hollow or rotten or

114

shaky or poor stuff; it had gone by, the same as an apple that has hung on the tree too long. When I was a boy my own father told me that there was more good timber then than in his young days when they was cutting trees and burning them for ashes. The old-growth hemlocks would be four or five feet through, all right, but they was hollow, with just a little shell on the outside. Sometimes they had hollows big enough for a man to get into.

They burned culls for their potash, and respected good timber trees.

Of course there was an occasional big tree that was sound; you've heard real-estate agents talk about wide board flooring. And there's a door in John Gale's shop made out of one board.

John Gale's mother and grandfather had their cider-brandy distillery about two hundred yards west of his shop—the Guilford Mineral Springs Distillery. Cider brandy was quite an industry around here a hundred, a hundred thirty years ago.

John Gale told me how his folks used to make it then. First the cider fermented, and become hard cider. Then his mother and her men would put the hard cider in a forty-gallon iron kettle, which was fitted with a copper dome that had a pipe leading off to the worm. The worm was a spiral tube that could be cooled with water. They started a fire under the kettle, and watched it very closely. The moment it started to boil they would draw the fire just as quickly as they could, and let it cool. Then they would start a slow fire, and simmer off the run of brandy, as they called it. They ran it through once, and throwed the rest away. If they didn't draw the fire, the still would blow up: the cider would froth up like boiling sugar, and blow the top off the kettle.

The first run that come out of the still was what they called stouts, and it was a different quality than

the regular run. The last that run out would be weak, so they used to blend it with the stouts. The liquor was colorless by nature, so they would burn sugar in an iron skillet, and keep stirring it until it was a burned molasses. That was caramel color, and a few drops would color the brandy.

The brandy was run into barrels. The barrels was rolled on one side in the upper part of the distillery until the revenue officer came. They rolled in what they wanted to pay revenue on. The revenue man was supposed to know what the capacity of the distillery was, and about how much brandy would come off of that amount of cider. He checked the barrels, and they paid the revenue, and the barrels was stamped. Then they could be sold.

Along with skill, the cider-brandy business needed a feeling for public relations—only in those days they called it see-for-yourself.

They sold, all right. By the barrel. One time the revenue man didn't believe the Gales was showing as much of the product as they should; he thought the capacity of the still was a good deal more than the results they was getting. So they told him to run out the batch that was in the still, and see for himself how much they got.

He wasn't an expert, because he didn't draw the fire. The thing blew up, and they had a timber propped up on top of the dome, and the timber pushed right through the roof. They lost the whole forty gallons of cider.

The next time the revenue man came it was the

116

same fellow, and he just didn't see three or four finished barrels that was right staring him in the face.

One odd thing about cider, more people make it at home now than they ever did then, because almost all the mills is gone. Every fall you find one or two more of the old ones has shut down. So if you want cider, you've almost got to make it for yourself.

Rag carpets was another small industry in Vernon at one time. Hooked rugs are quite common; they was something women made at home in their spare time; but the old-fashioned rag carpet was another thing. It was beat up on a loom, and not everybody had one. The rags were cut into narrow strips, sewed end to end, and put on a shuttle. The loom worked by hand, but it throwed the shuttle for you. When you pulled the beater back, it would cuff the shuttle through between the threads; then you brought the beater down again, to pound up what you had just run through; draw the beater back, and it would kick the shuttle to the opposite side again. The beater had a sort of bracket with an arm on it that slid the shuttle. If the shuttle didn't go clear across, you sometimes had to finish poking it through for yourself.

Saving rags to make carpets on a neighborhood loom.

117

Some staples he
traded for at
the general store.

Salt and one or two staples like that Gramp might
have to buy at the general store. I doubt if general
stores has changed much since Gramp's time, except
maybe they take more pride now in the variety of
junk they carry. A fellow up the West River near
Williamsville had a story about him in some big
magazine; it told how he always had everything anybody could think of, and one day on a bet a man
asked him if he had a pulpit for sale. He poked around
in the shed until he found one. In Gramp's day people
was too busy to spend very much time making that
kind of bets.

Naturally Gramp could get things even at the store
without paying cash. He might work it out—lots of
people did that for Mr. Brasor down to Algiers clear
up to and after the second world war. Or he might
bring him produce or timber or anything else the
storekeeper figured he could use. Maybe that's why
we generally talk about going downstreet to do our
trading, instead of our shopping.

You hear talk nowadays about inflation. It couldn't
have made very much headway under the old system
where a man would pay for the use of his neighbor's
hayrake with a gallon of syrup. One neighbor of mine
bought all his potatoes from the same farmer, and he
always allowed him two dollars a bushel, whether the
going price was fifty cents or six dollars. I don't know
but what I'd like to see him in as Secretary of the
Treasury.

Of course the one shop that meant more to Gramp
than all the rest put together was the blacksmith's.
Even in his old age he could never get out of the
habit of picking up every bent nail or scrap of iron,
and throwing it into an old keg. I asked him one
time why he saved them. He said, "I might want
them some time, but I don't think so."

When he was a young fellow he used to take those scraps to the blacksmith. The blacksmith would take one of the larger pieces, and hammer it out kind of flat. Then he would take the scraps, little small pieces, lay them on top, and put them all in the forge. He would pound them all together, with some welding compound, a special sand, for a flux. He would keep on hammering it all together until he got quite a sizable piece of iron from the bent nails Gramp had saved up. After that he could shape it any way he wanted to.

It was quite a tedious job; most of the forges had nothing but charcoal fires, and of course hand bellowses. The smith mostly had some boy that he was teaching, and the boy worked the bellows and was also the striker. The apprentice was always the striker; while he was learning to shoe oxen, he had to prepare everything, and the big boss done the nailing on. The striker got his name from the job he had on large pieces of iron like a cart axle. When the iron come out of the forge, it would cool before the blacksmith could hit it. So the striker had a heavy hammer, and stood on the opposite side of the anvil. He struck the iron with a hard blow, and the black-

The smith and his striker shape the iron.

119

smith struck it with a soft blow that smoothed it up as they went along. If they wanted to draw out a piece of iron, the striker would hit it the heavy blow, and the blacksmith would beat the striker's hammer-marks out.

Shoeing oxen was a big part of the blacksmith's business; oxen wasn't shod just for the summer, but if they worked in the winter they was shod. It's harder work to shoe oxen than horses. In the first place the ox's hoof is divided, so there is two shoes go on each foot. Besides, oxen won't hold still. You have to put them into a stanchion, a special frame with belly bands to go under the ox, and a windlass to hoist him up. His feet have to be strapped down to a framework so he can't yank. There was one of those racks in Oscar Howe's shop up to Brattleboro until maybe thirty years ago.

Shoes for oxen and horses were turned out of bar iron, and chain was forged a link at a time.

Of course the old-time blacksmith always turned his own shoes out of bar iron; I've heard that when somebody in York State invented a horseshoe machine, it was one of the big things in winning the Civil War, and the Confederates sent some men up to Canada to sneak down and steal the plans. Maybe they was the same fellows that organized the St. Albans raid up at the other end of Vermont.

Besides turning his own shoes, the blacksmith could put in his spare time making nails and chain. Welding chain one link at a time is quite a job. They generally made the links separately, and then they would take two links, and put in an extra one to connect them, and so on. To shape a link they would make a blank, and turn it on a small anvil that was used for the purpose. This was a small anvil horn that fit in the main part; it tapered out smaller, so that they could work the links down just as small as they liked.

Making nails was originally done more by eye; they just hammered them out with a blob on top for a head, and a point on the other end. At that, you can see why so many old houses and pieces of furniture are pegged and not nailed. Later on they had a nail machine, which really amounted to a mold. They would buy nail bars commercially; they heated the bar, put in in the form and pounded it to a point; then they would cut the nail off, and shape the head. That was the last of the handmade nails; in Gramp's time they still just took any piece of wrought iron that someone brought in.

A blacksmith could make nails, repair axe heads, or invent a new tool, and his shop was a favorite hangout.

Saving iron went so far that they would even get the blacksmith to put a new bit into an axe. The axe head was iron, and the bit was a piece of steel set in for a cutting edge. When the steel was worn down, the blacksmith would split the head from the eye out, and put in a new piece of steel. Then the owner would take it home again and hang it—put in his own special helve.

The steel square was invented at a blacksmith shop right here in Vermont. You may not think it's an invention worth talking about, because what else would you make a carpenter's square out of? Well, the old squares was wood. This blacksmith upcountry used a wooden square to mark off hot iron, and the wood used to burn; so he conceived the idea of taking a broken saw blade, and welding on the short piece that was broken off to make a right angle. This was the first steel square that was ever made, and it got to be quite an industry in Vermont before other people started manufacturing them too.

Naturally the blacksmith was a real standby of the whole community. The men used to hang out there, the same as they would in the general store. One day when Gramp was sitting around the blacksmith shop

121

in Vernon, he offered to bet that he could drive a tenpenny nail into a board farther with one blow of his hand than what the blacksmith could with one blow of his hammer. Gramp was pretty well along in years, and it seemed like a foolish kind of bet anyway; in the end the whole village of Vernon got so excited that they had to try it out instead of just talking about it.

Naturally the blacksmith knew he could win, but still he was kind of afraid he might hit his fingers with the big sledgehammer. He took it careful, like, and all the loafers begun to wonder a little if he would win after all.

Gramp wound a bandanna around his hand, grabbed the nail in his fist with the head against his palm, and slammed it right through the board with all his might.

When they come to measure the nails, they decided Gramp wasn't quite such a foolish old man as they supposed.

122

CHAPTER 9

Around the House

I EXPECT this ought to be more about Grandma than about Grandpa, only I never knew her so well, and I always think of Gramp baching it when he was bringing me up. I guess he had a right to be thought of as around the house at that, considering how many of them he helped frame.

When the frame was raised, and the house was roofed and sheathed and clapboarded, they might paint it if they was real proud of it. They would have to go down to the store for some powdered red ochre, a color they call Venetian red now; but the rest of it they done themselves. They mixed the red with buttermilk or whey from cheese. Buttermilk red is the characteristic color on really old houses and furniture around these parts. It couldn't fade, any more than a dead man could die, because it had gone down

Antiques here are buttermilk red.

to its last element; it was really an iron rust gone down to its last rust. That is why these old houses stay red forever.

After the red paint come white lead. Occasionally you see a house in Windham County painted what some people call Colonial yellow, with the old yellow ochre; but it was nearly all red or white.

Oil paints come in fairly early; there was plenty of linseed oil around here. Gramp used to mix it with red ochre, what he called turkey red, and paint it on metal or spots that had weathered off. As a young man he would use bass-bark brushes, so he didn't have to go to the store even for them. By my time he used store brushes, and he had a paint mill that I used to run. It was a little iron mill something like a meat-grinder, only it turned around like a millstone. You fed fat skins and old dried-up scraps and dregs of different-colored paint into the top, and reground them into fat paints, with turkey red to drown out all the other shades.

After the paint was reground, it come out so thick and heavy that it was almost like a paste. Gramp used to let it down with turpentine and oil. I wouldn't recommend the job of grinding paint by hand to anybody; I found it took quite a long time to get anything done.

You remember how the first job Gramp give me was to paint the cellar door and teach me not to argue with the man I was working for. Later on he showed me the secret of painting. The formula was to brush it on, brush it in, and brush it out. You brush the paint on, brush it in on the rough places, and brush it out to make it go as far as you can. I followed the trade of painting for several years, and I never found any better way of doing it. That's still how you paint a barn.

124

Those old oil paints used to last all right. John Gale's barn was painted the year Cleveland was elected, with nothing but red ochre and oil, the battens painted white. It's still red and white just the same as it was then, and the same paint job.

Still a good paint job.

Gramp made his own paint, and he made his own butternut dye, and he also made his own harness- or shoe-blacking, and his own ink. For harness-blacking, he saved up his saw filings, and dissolved them in vinegar. Leather dressing, for use instead of looks, was lampblack and tallow. Gramp always had lampblack in a little old can; he would take a fat pine knot, get it burning in the stove, and then hold it under a piece of metal to collect the smoke. Afterward he would scrape the lampblack off into the can.

As long as he lived he always made his own ink. The base was saw filings and vinegar, the same as for harness-blacking; then he would put in a little white maple bark to get tannic acid to make the ink more permanent. The vinegar ate up the saw filings, and made the color. That kind of ink turns light brown with age—iron rust is what it turns to; you've seen some of these old letters. Originally the ink was black.

Making his ink and cutting pens.

He used steel pens in my time, but I've seen him make a quill pen, the same as he done when he was younger. It's quite a trick; it takes a very sharp knife and pretty good eyesight. Gramp cut the quill off at a slant, scraped out the pith, and then split it up the long side. If he didn't quite get it centered, he would have to work it down until the two points

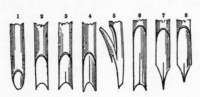

come even. It sounds simple enough, but it has to be well done in order to make a pen that will write much of any.

Pens was cut from goose quills, and Gramp generally had a few geese. I don't remember much about them except the old gander used to make my legs black and blue; he was always biting me and slapping me with his wings. They kept the geese for quills and feather beds and feather pillows and suchlike, but most stuffings was hen feathers. Everybody slept on cornhusk ticks with feather beds on top; I never see a mattress until I was quite a young man.

Of course the ticks rested on cord beds. Instead of a bedspring with slats underneath, they had cord strung between the bed rails. It practically took a mechanic to put a cord bed together; the ropes was laced back and forth crisscross, and after a while they would stretch out and sag down. Then you took a bed key, a two-inch square block about a foot and a half long, with a slot cut into one end to catch the rope, and a wooden crossbar at the other end to give you leverage; you give a twist and pulled up the slack in the ropes one at a time until they was taut again.

Gramp used to braid a lot of stuff, mainly rawhide and such as that, but the cordage for beds and farm work was mostly brought in from the ropewalks, and was very much prized. All the ropewalks was near the coast, on account of rigging ships; a lot of the cordage come in from Boston. Ropes was taken care of pretty choicely, and anything that come tied up with string, Gramp would save the string and wind it up in a ball.

For guests and big occasions they would put homespun linen sheets on the bed; they made their own linen, so they didn't think much of it. In fact one of

Feather beds on cornhusk ticks.

Rope was choice, but linen couldn't compare with his cotton shirt.

126

Gramp's favorite expressions for anything extra nice was, "as fine as a cotton shirt." He generally wore wool flannel shirts and wool underwear, and a cotton shirt to him was just about as nice as it could be.

After they had cut and dried the flax, they would soak it to rot the outer husk; then they put it through a flax-breaker, which is two big timbers hinged at

the far end, and shaped into two heavy wooden blades that drop into slots in the lower timber. They would work the blades up and down to crush the outside shell of the flax, and the fibers wouldn't break. Then they drew the fibers through a hetchel—a bunch of long, sharp spikes set into a plank. They would take a fistful of flax, and keep drawing it through until the finer part of the husk was combed out. Then they carded the flax with wide cards, something like a currycomb—wires, instead of spikes like the hetchel, set upright in a board with a handle.

Fiber was broken and carded, then spun into hard thread on a flax wheel.

Finally they would spin it into thread. The flax wheel is the small wheel, run with a treadle, not kicked ahead by hand or with a dolly like the wool wheels. The small flax wheel would run the spindle faster, and spin the flax into a hard thread, whereas the wool was to be spun rather loose, into more of a yarn.

The loom would weave either linen or wool; the

127

difference was merely the harness and combs that they used. The combs was the set of little slats where the threads of the warp run through. And of course for wool the shuttle had to be bigger. As I remember it, Gramp's family used to do their own spinning, but go to a neighbor for the weaving. There was likely to be just one family in a neighborhood that had a loom, and done the weaving for everybody.

Cloth had to be pretty rugged in Gramp's time to stand the washing it got. All Grandmother could do to it was either beat it with a stick or use soft soap, and if she used soft soap she pretty well had to beat it too. People complain about what laundries do to clothes now, but I bet it isn't much worse than what would have happened to fancy modern clothes in the old days. Soft soap was stored in a special barrel downcellar, and I can tell you a soft-soap barrel didn't last too long. The lye would eat the wood until it became all soft. If Gramp was fixing a barrel for soap he made the staves good and heavy, so as to have them last at least for a while.

For washing your hands, they had a dish that sat around. You just dipped in there, got one hand soapy, and went to it. It was kind of a soupy mess, like the liquid soap you find in washrooms, only it wasn't quite so refined. There was some hard soap made, but it took more and better lye, and was more work to make. Gramp never bothered with it.

I mentioned before that the other side of my family for four generations was directly connected with soap through making potash. Grandfather Needham used to buy up all the ashes of the neighborhood, and leach them through big vats. That would give him lye water that he'd boil down to make a crude potash. Grandfather Needham would sell the leached-out ashes themselves for fertilizer, and then refine the

128

potash into pearlash for soap. It was partly because of people like him that the old fireplaces had an ash pit at one side below the oven. Instead of sprinkling ashes on icy paths or using them in the outhouse, they saved them up carefully for the potashmaker. Supposedly the first American patent was issued on July 31, 1790, to Samuel Hopkin of Burlington, Vermont, for a special way of leaching ashes to make potash.

Ranges must have come in before Gramp was very old, but during his boyhood the fireplace was the main thing in the kitchen. Of course there was a crane to hang kettles on. The brass kettles, of various sizes, was kind of dress-up kettles; the iron kettles were the everyday ones. They had legs, so they would either set on the hearth next to the fire, or hang by a pothook on the crane. The frying pan was more or less like a warming pan except that it was iron, with an iron cover that could be fitted on to it, and an iron handle about three feet long so that you could fish it out of the fire. There wasn't too much stuff fried then, though; things was mostly either cooked on a spit or in a pot.

His mother cooked in the fireplace before cast-iron wood ranges came along.

Don't make the same mistake a lot of people do, and call the brick oven next to the fireplace a Dutch oven. The brick ovens at the side was used for baking bread.

Such baking was a kind of a weekend affair. They would build up a fire in the fireplace, and when

they got a lot of hot coals they would shovel them into the oven, and close it up; usually there was sort of an unhinged door or lid of wrought iron. After quite a while, when the oven felt right, they would shovel the coals out and into the ash pit under the oven. They would slide the bread and beans in with wooden shovels, called peels. The coals in the pit helped to keep the bottom of the oven warm, and of course in the end they was shoveled out and sold for potash. Heating the oven and baking took so long that they only done it once a week.

Places like the old Liberty Pole Tavern that John Gale's grandfather run had to heat a lot of water, so there would be an arch kettle built right in on one side of the fireplace. The arch was generally fired from inside the house, and you had a door that opened out into the shed; you could reach out and bail hot water from outside the partition. The kettle would hold maybe forty gallons.

For a winter evening's hobby up to the time his teeth got bad, instead of eating popcorn Gramp would eat parched corn. He used to parch it for me too. He would dry sweet corn, and then soak it, and finally parch it in the oven. He would stir it around while it was roasting in the range oven, and it would come out a little bit like roasted peanuts. It took quite a lot of jaw power to eat it, but it tasted pretty good.

Parched corn, raw turnip, and boiled cider for treats.

After his teeth was gone he used to eat raw turnip—take a knife, cut the purple top off, and scrape the inside so it was a pulp that he could eat.

Another delicacy was boiled cider, which was about all they really used the brass kettles for. Grandmother would take sweet cider immediately before it started to work, and boil it down to the thickness of syrup; in fact you might say it was a kind of sour molasses. Generally she put it in mincemeat, and it was supposed to be extra special.

Water on the farm is like the seasons: you don't think about it until after you've bought your first farm and spent a dry summer there. Somebody told me once that lack of water was the biggest thing that held up the growth of Los Angeles in its early days. It would hold up the growth of a farm, all right. Luckily we have a lot of water in our part of Vermont, and Gramp was good at finding it. He always claimed that he could do water-witching—detect running water with a forked stick. He showed me how to do it, but it won't work with me; I haven't the confidence. I can make it look like it was working, and that's all.

You cut a crotch of apple or witch hazel about the thickness of your little finger, with prongs maybe two feet long. Some dowsers use peach when they're witching, and some use maple, and I claim you can do it with any stick that has a good crotch on it; but apple and witch hazel seem to be the favorites. You turn your palms up, and take the end of a prong in each hand, with the point of the crotch straight upward. Then you walk around, and if you pass over running water the point of the stick is supposed to dip toward the ground so hard you can't stop it.

To me the trouble is that if you put the tension on your muscles just right and bend up on the ends a little, the stick will kink and drop, and even break the bark when it twists if you're holding on tight. It will happen anywhere, nothing to do with water, even if you don't move your hands. There's nothing I can find in science that would indicate there is any attraction between the earth and the stick if it has water under it or if it hasn't. There is water

Dowsing for water is up to the man, not the stick.

131

under it anyway, at some depth, and I just can't convince myself that the stick knows anything about it.

Gramp found plenty of water, but then of course he knew where to go and dig some up without any stick. He found water generally by the lay of the land. He would watch the moist places and the water that worked out of the ground in the spring; he would see how long it stayed there. And he went by geology, too, the same as I do when I'm looking for water; he would note how the ledges run, and spot the swamps that he figured the water oozed out of from the ground.

After Gramp found water, if it wasn't a big spring, he would have to dig a well. That was a two-man job after he got down a little way. The hole to start with would be quite large, depending on how deep they thought they was going, but generally ten or twelve feet across. When it got down to where they had trouble throwing the dirt over and out, they started another hole in the center or to one side, a smaller size, and dug down again. They would throw the dirt on to the shelf, and the next man would relay it up; they throwed it up with long spades. Possibly they might have to make as many as two shelves. Most wells are not much over twenty foot deep; you hear of forty-foot wells, but I never see one. Around here twenty-five is a good well. If they didn't begin to strike water by then, I don't know what they would have done—dug somewhere else, most likely.

When they hit water, sometimes it would be in a sand vein so that they would have to box it in, because the sand would keep caving. They would take planks to hold the mud out until they could start laying up the bottom of the hole.

Laying up a well was an art all to itself, like build-

A twenty-five-foot well was dug with long spades, and a helper stood midway down the hole to relay dirt to the top.

132

ing stone walls, only the stones for laying a well was selected. They had to be of about a uniform size and tapering at one end, like a keystone. Gramp would lay the well with the pointed ends of the stones toward the center of the well. That made the circular form, and then when the dirt pressed against them from behind, they could never fall in. It's very seldom you see an old well that has caved.

The science of laying up a well.

As Gramp built up, somebody would shovel down the dirt and odd-shaped rocks against the outside of the stone well. They worked the dirt in and packed it down as they went along, and when they got through the well was there for good.

Pumps on wells is a comparatively new idea. In Gramp's time they first had a long wooden well-sweep with a permanent bucket attached to the end; you poured the water from that into another bucket that you brought with you from the house. By the time I come along they had got a windlass instead of a sweep. Later on they just had a hook on a chain, hooked the bucket on, and threw it down the well. They hauled up the pail of water, and took it away with them.

Then I know where there's an old wooden suction pump, all wood except the bottom valve, which is a piece of old boot leather with a chunk of lead on it. As long as they had to depend on them things, I don't know but what a bucket was less work.

Water and the time of year was a lot more important to Grandpa than the exact time of day. He owned a watch when I knew him, but he seldom carried it unless he was dressed up. After you live in a locality forty or fifty years, you get to know the points of the compass pretty accurately, and Gramp would merely hold up something and look at the shadow to tell

133

the time of day. The noon shadow will point due north, and he could judge the angle at other hours.

Telling time on a windowsill in the kitchen.

When Grandmother was fixing to get dinner, she went by the sun-mark that Gramp had scratched on the corner of the southerly kitchen windowsill. It was the same idea as a sundial—a diagonal line sloping inward from the outer edge of the frame. When the shadow fell on the mark, Grandma knew it was noon. There was two marks, one for summer and one for winter. Neither one of them was much good on a cloudy day.

They had a clock, too, with wooden works, which had to be cranked up every night. I never was allowed to wind it. You had to insert a small crank in the face of the clock, and wind up the weights, one on each side, one for time and one for striking. The clock was probably two foot high, tall enough for the weight to come down. There was a looking glass in the lower half.

The glass was the main thing about the clock to Gramp, because he used it when he shaved. I still have his Joseph Elliot razor; the blade was imported, but the handle is native oak wood. It will still give you the best shave you ever had, even if it does weigh five pounds and look something like a meat-cleaver.

He was shaving one day in a thunderstorm, and the lightning struck the Balm of Gilead tree, and come into the house, and knocked the clock down. It smashed the glass and left Gramp half shaved.

Gramp died before I went off to the first world war, but he lived long enough to see some new inventions that was faster than the old ways, only they never struck him as quite so dependable. He always thought automobiles was a good way of getting around—some better than going with oxen or shanks' mare; but

134

he never cared much about them. They was more
of a joke to him than anything else. Automobiles
all run on benzene in those days and smelled pretty
strong. One time he come out in the morning, and
the air was frowy with skunk, and he said it smelled
like an automobile had been by.

I know for a fact he couldn't make head or tail
out of a telephone as long as he lived. He never knew
which was the receiver and which was the sending
end. I remember once when he was over to our house
the phone rang 1–4. He'd been told that was our
ring, and he knew you had to lift the black thing
off the fork. He done that all right, and something
squawked hello at him. He listened to one end and
then the other, and yelled "What?" into the receiver,
and finally something said hello again, kind of im-
patient, and Gramp tried yelling "What?" in the
mouthpiece for a change, and the people at the other
end said, "Hello, is this Needham's?"

Gramp thought he had done something to get
an answer, but right away he forgot and tried the
receiver again.

Finally he hollered for me so loud you'd have
thought I had put one of his saws back on the wrong
peg in the shop.

Encounter with that thing on the wall.

135

CHAPTER 10.

Indians

GRAMP is the only man I ever knew, or knew of, that actually helped an Indian collect herbs for Kickapoo Indian medicine. People generally think Kickapoo Indian medicine was just water and burnt sugar, as Indian as you are, merely something to sell for a dollar a bottle at medicine shows. Maybe most of it was, but Gramp made the real thing.

He was probably fifteen or sixteen—old enough to be full of questions—when this old Kickapoo doctor came down the river from the north, looking for herbs. Gramp was interested, and used to go with him. The Indian was looking for some particular herb, and showed Gramp what it was.

He knew a real medicine man.

Gramp happened to know where there was a lot of it, so he took the old Indian over. After that the old fellow came there often for different herbs, because he found so many. After a while it got so that this old Indian would show him an herb, tell him what it was and when it should be gathered, and ask Gramp to pull some up for him and save it until he could come, because he wouldn't be there at the right season.

So Gramp learned a great many of these herbs, and what the uses were, and how to prepare some of the different concoctions. I wish I hadn't forgotten so much of it; and besides I suppose Gramp didn't tell me all about it, at that.

He did tell me about the Kickapoo doctor curing somebody of tapeworm. He crushed up punkin seeds, and boiled them, and give the fellow the water to drink. Fixed him right up, too.

Punkin seeds cure worms; and looking for poplar buds.

The principal part of my job with the herbs was to collect the buds from Balm of Gilead poplar. When the buds start to swell in the spring they are filled with a sort of pitch, and if you go around where there is Balm of Gilead poplar you will smell them. It smells like medicine. They grew a good deal on his farm in Vernon; they're kind of a weed tree, and will spring up anywhere. They're not considered anything for fuel or lumber; to the average person they wouldn't look much different from any popple tree.

I used to have to gather the swelling buds, and then Gramp would dry them. Some of them he would just put fresh in a pint bottle, and when the bottle was full of buds he poured it full of grain alcohol and left it to soak. That made a liniment, and he even claimed it was good for colic.

He used most of the buds in his hard salve, and in soft salve or ointment. For the hard salve he would send me out to collect white-pine pitch. If

Balm of Gilead in liniment or salve.

137

there was any white-pine lumber around, that was the best source to get the pitch. I would scrape it off the end of boards and logs with an old knife and get it into a can. I put the can on the stove, and melted and strained the pitch. Once it was strained through cheesecloth, just enough to take the sawdust and bark out, the pitch from off of logs or lumber would look like the nicest basswood honey you ever saw.

White-pine pitch for hard salve.

Next Gramp put the pitch on the stove where it wouldn't be too hot, and boiled it down slowly until it would form a rosin in cold water; I used to get some of it to chew for gum. Then he cooked up a mixture of the rosin, mutton tallow, and Balm of Gilead buds. He strained it and poured it in molds—tins, or anything he could get. Mostly he'd try to make it into sticks, like sealing wax.

He used the hard salve on the oxen. When they wore shoes in winter, they would sometimes cut one foot with the other shoe. Gramp would take a match and warm the end of a salve stick to the melted stage, and put some on the cut. It would coat right over and stay there. When I had cracks in my hands from chaps, he would warm hard salve at the fire, and drop a little in the cracks. There it hardened again to form a protective coating, and it was really healing.

Sure protection, and healing too.

The soft salve was an ointment to rub on. It was made without the boiled-down pine pitch—just mutton tallow and Balm of Gilead, and I think sometimes he used butter in it. It was very good stuff.

Sometimes butter in his ointment.

Gramp was always telling me the medical properties of different plants in the woods, such as pipsissewa and sarsaparilla and rattlesnake plantain, which he called the king of all poisons. It is a beautiful little plant, but I never tried it out to see if he was right about the poison.

Sarsaparilla and sassafras root was used in making root beer. When I was very small he made root beer occasionally, but later years he didn't bother. He also made hop beer. Then his male hop plant died, and so they was all pulled up. Hops has to be of each kind, one male plant set in the center with four or five of the female vines around it. When the male vine dies there will be no more hops.

Sassafras root or hops for beer.

The herb I know best about is wild turnip or jack-in-the-pulpit. Gramp used to give it to me to start a sweat or cure my cold, and I can tell you it did.

Jack-in-the-pulpit to stop a cold.

You watch the plants until the berries get ripe or the plant goes to seed. When the berries are red it's right to gather. You pull up the bulbs, and peel them, and put them where they will dry. Once they are dry they're good to keep indefinitely, the same as any spice.

In the winter when you have a chill or are coming down with a cold or grippe or fever, you grate one level teaspoonful of that jack-in-the-pulpit bulb, and mix it up in hot water with milk and sugar. Maple or white sugar, it doesn't make any difference. It's not unpleasant to take, but you certainly will warm up. I think it is equal to Jamaica ginger or anything of that sort. If I was going to prescribe it, I would go a little bit lighter on the ingredients.

Leaf tobacco (which they used to grow a good deal in Vernon), smartweed, and mullein was used for poultices to create a local irritation. If you wanted to warm up any injured place, you would make a poultice out of the mullein leaves and smartweed. Smartweed grows wild around here, and looks so much like heartsease that you can scarcely tell them apart unless you handle the smartweed or get it in

Three plants good in poultices.

139

your eyes. If you look close at heartsease you can see a very faint black form of a heart in the leaf; that's a pleasanter way to tell the difference.

Teas for fever.

Grandpa always gathered tansy and pennyroyal and catnip to brew up with water for tea. Most all of his herb mixtures was some kind of a brew. He used to make catnip tea and tansy tea for mild fevers or to give to children.

Beef-gall pellets were laxative.

When the beef was butchered, Gramp would save the gall in an earthenware bowl, and dry it down to a black gummy mess that looked a good deal like tar, only not quite so black. For a laxative he would dig out a little of this gummy stuff, and roll it up in a round pellet not quite the size of a Canada pea or a field pea; that was one dose. It was about the size of any pill, except it wasn't sugar-coated, and believe me it was bitter: I've taken them.

Hickory-nut oil as a substitute fat.

An Indian product that Gramp told me about but never made was hickory-nut oil. The Indians used it as a substitute for mother's milk or fats of any kind. They done that quite often with butternuts, too. They would take a hollow stump, fill it with hickory nuts, and pound them into a meal with a stone pestle; then they filled the stump with water and put in hot stones out of the fire. The oil raised to the top, and the shucks stayed on the bottom.

They quite often boiled fish the same way; cooked it with hot stones in a wooden trencher or a clay pot until the meat come off and the bones settled to the bottom.

Gramp used to tell me stories of the various things the Indians made, and how they would catch and spear fish. They came to the Connecticut River for the salmon run and the shad run some time in the spring. They always went to the rapids or falls, and

140

they would generally camp below if there was a suitable place. They always picked their campgrounds where there was clean water and a flat space around it.

The method of spearing salmon was to take a dugout canoe and go up above the falls. When the fish had managed to get up the falls or rapids they were very tired, and it was no trouble at all just to reach over the side and spear them, and bring them into the dugouts. When the fishermen got carried downstream close to the rapids they stopped and threw the fish ashore. The squaws cleaned them and smoked them, and the men went back for another haul.

The men speared and trapped fish coming upriver to spawn, while the squaws smoked the catch or used it to fertilize each hill of corn.

The shad they used to catch mostly in weirs made out of willow. They would cut willow sticks and set them around in the shallows, hoping to get anything into it that they could. The weirs was quite often built near places where the Indians was going to raise corn or their summer crops, because what they didn't eat they used for fertilizer. Fish of a certain size, or a certain amount of fish, went into every hill of corn.

Instead of plowing the cornfields like we do, the Indians burned them over every year. In most of the flat places where I find Indian relics, there's a black line at one level of the soil, and under a glass you see that it's tiny pieces of charcoal.

Canoes was an important subject to the Indians, and most people have some wrong ideas about them. The birchbark canoe was a wonderful piece of construction, but it wasn't as popular as the dugout, and it was sort of a makeshift. A tribe would travel regularly from up north down to the coast over the same route every year, back and forth. The dugouts was kept on the trails, and the Indians would take one dugout as far as a stream went; then, instead of portaging it to the next stream, they would fill the canoe full of stones and bury it in the wet mud. At the next stream they would dig up another dugout, and take that as far as it would go. A white-pine dugout, if it was kept under water, would last probably the life of a man, just like a pumplog.

White-pine dugouts could be buried by the trail from year to year.

They made their dugouts from old-growth pine. They would build fires on the log, and burn it and scrape it out with stone adzes. Once they got through the sapwood, the pine would char quite easily. They would work out several pits, and what impressed Grandpa specially was the skillful way they left cross sections in to brace the sides of the canoe, to make it strong enough for any kind of a current or load. The dugouts would run up to forty feet long, but they must have been narrow.

The paper-birch canoes was used on journeys that were not annual. They couldn't be buried, but of course you could make a portage with one. Gramp showed me how the Indians used to take measurements with two sticks for the framework of a birch canoe. You hold two sticks together side by side. To measure any distance longer than one of the sticks, you pull one stick out to project the correct distance beyond the other, and hold the two that way while you transfer the measure.

Their only tool for building a birchbark canoe.

The Indians made their birch canoes with neither

142

hammer, square, saw, nor any kind of measure except the two sticks and their eye. For the framework they laid poles out on the ground in the shape they wanted the gunwales, and drove stakes to hold the poles in the proper curve. Next they bent the ribs, lashed them on to the gunwale poles, and built the skeleton frame of the canoe bottom-side up. Then they put on the birchbark skin, and lashed it with tamarack roots, and finally they pitched the seams with spruce gum. The marvel of it to Gramp was that the first time the canoe was set in the water it would ride on an even keel, and be perfect.

Gramp was always telling me the ways of the Indians making different things, like bows and arrows, and how straight they could shoot. He even made me a bow and arrow one time. The first thing I done was shoot a cat with it, and I got a licking with the bow afterwards.

How Gramp made me a bow and arrow by Indian methods.

He made the bow of a hemlock limb, shaved down a very little on the small end, and naturally more on the thick end; it was shaved only on the inside. It was very powerful. The arrow was the dried stalk of a cattail flag. The end of this one was wound with stout thread around a nail that was filed down; of course the Indians used stone points. Mine was feathered with ordinary hen feathers instead of crow feathers, but it would shoot very straight. You take a wing feather, and strip it down from the top on the wide side; you lash two of those opposite each other with regular shoe thread or harness thread—just two. The American Indians never used but two feathers. The butt was notched, but it also had to be wound; the top lashing of the feathers acted as a reinforcement for the notch so that the bowstring wouldn't split it.

The Indians was like any careful workmen about

their arrowheads; they had different types for different things. There was one for big game, with a heavy point. The bird points was supposed to be small. They made their war arrows in the shape of a V, without a shank, and worked them down thin where the shaft goes on, as well as sharp around the edges. They were lashed loose enough on the shaft so that if they struck a person, and he pulled out the arrow, the point would be left inside him to create fever.

War arrow points had a special shape and purpose.

The New England Indians didn't use poisoned arrows, but they did have a poison that they got from pokeberry. Pokeberry is a pretty-looking berry that makes a nice vermilion stain; it's also called inkberry. Grandpa told me if you took the roots and boiled them, and soaked corn in it, it would poison crows; but he said it was kind of a dirty trick, and I never see him do it.

Gramp said the Indians would shoot half as far as a good gun—maybe up to fifty or seventy-five yards. I suppose an arrow at that distance would be pretty well spent; it would depend a lot on the heft of the head. Some of the Indian bows was about five feet long, which would give you a good pull. The bow he made me was almost as tall as I was, about four feet long. I thought it was too big, but I found I could draw it.

I don't know how the Indians would have stood up against fellows in storybooks like Robin Hood, but they could shoot pretty straight; they even put arrows through squirrels and pigeons. I don't suppose they hit them every time.

Arrows, specially the heads, represented a lot of work, and the Indians would retrieve all they possibly could. Every Indian had his own totem or mark so he could claim his arrows. If there was any others

They signed each arrow so its owner could claim it.

144

turned up in battle, of course he retrieved those too.

If you'd seen as many stone arrowheads as I have, and tried making them yourself, you'd agree that it was pretty wonderful how the Indians could sit down with no metal tools, and make hundreds of stone points that are all almost identical in design, one after another.

You naturally think of flint and arrowheads together, but they are not necessarily all flint; around here they were made of quartz or any hard stone. Some of them in the far West are obsidian, and some are agate. The chief thing is to pick up a stone that will split or fracture in sheets or layers.

I have discovered from the chips and fragments I've found up and down the river that the Indians started their points exactly the same as a diamond cutter starts a diamond. They laid the quartz, or whatever it was, on another sharp stone, and struck it with something to cleave it and chip it. They put the sharp edge on by flaking off little bits evenly with a staghorn.

Starting a point was like cleaving a diamond, then a staghorn flaked bits off to give it sharp edges.

The good ones was sharp, all right. An Indian on the warpath wasn't anything you wanted to fool around with much. Newfane, the shire town of Windham County—where they had John Gale's old ward, the cut-up, in jail—is a real pretty village down in a valley off the West River. It has the county courthouse and the Grange and some other nice white clapboard buildings, and you'd think it had been there since the settlers took the land away from the Indians. It has, too—since just a few years before Gramp was born. The place where Newfane is now used to be called Fayetteville; Newfane was right up on top of Newfane Hill. You'd probably call Newfane Hill a mountain; it's pretty steep, even for these parts. Newfane was built up there for protection

145

from the Indians, and it would take almost a medium tank to attack the old site now.

Finally, in 1825, they decided the Indians wasn't going to bother them no more, and it really was a pretty smart climb up Newfane Hill, specially in mud time. So they built the courthouse in Fayetteville, then took apart most of the buildings on the hill and drawed them down by ox team, and set them around the green like they are now. Every so often somebody tries to move the shire town from Newfane to Brattleboro, but I don't think they'll ever succeed. It used to be one of John Gale's hobbies to stop them.

But his biggest hobby of all was the Indians. The last ten years of his life he and I spent almost every pleasant Sunday together, Indian-relicking. I suppose partly because Gramp had told me things about the Indians, I was the one found most of the stuff at first. Later on John done just as well as I did.

At that, I was long enough getting started. Gramp used to tell me about hoeing up arrow points down at Houghton's Ferry and on the Eli Clark farm up on Putney Road. Eli Clark was some relation by marriage, and he had an old stone house down by the river; it's still there. From the time Gramp told me about hoeing things up on that farm, I always had a great yen to find an arrow point. I looked for them all my life from the time I was big enough to scout around, only I didn't know how to look, or where to look, or what to look for.

Gramp's story ends here, and my own part begins.

This is about where we say goodbye to Gramp. He got me started on the Indians when I was small, and told me what he learned from his friend the Kickapoo doctor; the Indians before his time he didn't know so much about.

He died before I went off to war in 1917, and I'm

afraid you may think most of what he knew died with
him, to judge by how little I remember. The subject
of Indians is the only one that I've finally decided I
know more about than him, and it took me long
enough to find out so that I'm not very stuck up
about it. Anyway, these last few pages is from me,
not Grandpa Bond.

The first arrow point I ever found was right out
here opposite the Tyler Hill Road, up on the ledges.
I was about eighteen, and I'd been hunting ever
since I was a dozen years old. I was working for John
Gale then, the same as I did off and on until twenty
years ago, when he died. He gave me a dollar for
the arrow point, and he always wore it as a watch
fob. He cherished it because it was so snowy white,
and was found in Guilford. I'm sorry he never finished
his *History of Guilford,* but then I never thought he
would. It would have been a lot bigger than most
school histories of the United States. A committee got
out the *History* in 1961, using most of what he'd
written down, and his notes.

I went on hunting for relics right along, but I
didn't find no more for nearly twenty-five years. When
the Boston and Maine railroad was built on the
New Hampshire side of the river, more than fifty
years ago, some of the workmen would find relics,
so I used to swim the river and go looking; but I
still didn't find none.

Twenty-five years
between relics.

Finally, after the big flood of '36, John and I
went out fishing. We was looking for relics at the
same time. The fishing was as good as ever, but the
relicking was poor. There was a big washout on
the Vernon side of the Connecticut, with the bank
all chewed away to sand, and I went up in to look
it over.

In the sand I discovered some white flint chips or

quartz chips. They looked funny to me because there was no stone; it was all plain sand.

Then I run on to a mud-colored piece of clay pottery. I made up my mind that it wasn't anything I had seen before. I studied it for a few minutes, and finally concluded it was Indian pottery. I tied up a few pieces in my bandanna handkerchief, and took them right over to Mr. Gale. As long as the wash was on the Vermont side, that got him excited, and we started on our first big Indian-relic hunt. We combed that thirty acres of sand over and over.

I found out later that the pottery we found would be Algonquin. The art is all executed in straight lines, never a scroll. There's some handsome designs on the pieces, squares and little dots, but you never find a crooked mark. Evidently they was scraped with a shell, and mostly marked with a shell too. One particular piece I found was stamped all over with little twin dots, evidently made by the end of a split stick. As near as I could figure, it was to represent deer tracks. The tops were invariably crimped with thumbnail and finger, like some women crimp their pies; you can almost see the prints of the nails, although some of the pieces are well worn.

The things we found started John Gale studying old books that he could get hold of. He scared up an old history of Northfield, Massachusetts, giving a description of the corn cellars at South Vernon. He told me there used to be more corn stored in the Indian corn cellars at South Vernon than was being raised then in the whole of Windham County.

I said, "I know where those are."

He says, "It's on the riverbank, and I'd like to know just where—if it's in Vermont or Massachusetts."

I told him I didn't know which side of the line, but anyway it was on the Belden farm. The only thing

148

we had to go by was this book, but we went down there, and sure enough I walked straight to the Indian cellars.

Visiting
the corn cellars.

They are pits maybe ten feet square, dug at the foot of a bank, two of them side by side. The bottoms were evidently filled with clay and pounded hard, because there is no trees or brush growing on them even to this day, though they're right in the brush. The earth was thrown up a little around the outside. I suppose the corn was stacked in there, and covered over with something.

The cellars was first discovered by a party that come up the river from Deerfield, I suppose before this territory around here was settled—maybe in 1700 or so.

Offshore a ways upstream from the Belden farm is Pomeroy's Island, just below Vernon Dam. Lieutenant Pomeroy and another party was up from Deerfield in 1689, and they seen a couple of Indians in a canoe. They fired on the Indians, and the Indians tipped over and beat it. Pomeroy thought he would get the canoe, and when he started to, one of the Indians potted him. All Pomeroy got was an island named after his memory.

On the way out from the corn cellars, John Gale and I met the owner of the property; the land had been in the Belden family since Indian times. I told him what we had been looking at. He begun to laugh. "I was shown those by my father," he said, "and I went to show them to my daughter a week or two ago, and I couldn't find them."

As we went up and down the river, John told me what he had read in the book about the fort at Fort Hill, near the New Hampshire end of the Vernon Dam. So we went over there. It's a small round hill, probably not more than a hundred feet across the

The hill is small,
but it was ideal
for a fortress.

top. You can see from there to the mouth of Broad Brook or pretty near to Brattleboro, and you can see down the river about half a mile.

It was an Indian fortress. This old book said that they had a log stockade around the top of the hill, and a covered passage that went to the river. As near as we could find out, it was the only permanent location the Indians occupied here in this part of the state. Their land that they farmed was on the Vermont side in the bow of the river, and the fort was on the New Hampshire side. The bow of the river is the only place on the Connecticut where you can stand on the east side of the river and be on the west side, and face downstream and upstream without moving. For a few yards there, the river runs very nearly north. When you stand at the narrowest neck of the point, it isn't more than forty foot wide.

Tracing out Fort Hill's covered passage and earthworks.

When we went to Fort Hill we could follow traces of everything the book said was there. We found the covered passage, where the ground had sunk in; it came from a spring down on the riverbank, and zigzagged back and forth into the fort on top of the hill.

150

Then as a protection from the north, there was an earthworks that still stands anywhere from six inches to a foot high, and about eighteen inches thick. It follows all along the riverbank, probably a distance of a thousand yards, to the point where it was destroyed in building the dam. If hostile tribes came from the north, the local Indians could get behind this bank and shoot from there. On the south the bank was about sixty foot high. They had piles of logs at the top, and if the enemy started climbing the bank they would roll logs over, and mow them all down at once.

The historians used to say there was no signs of permanent Indian occupancy along the Connecticut in Vermont, but they're wrong. I've mentioned some of the things. Another thing, King Philip had a big powwow in Vernon after the famous raid on Lancaster, Massachusetts, when Mrs. Mary White Rowlandson was carried away captive. In her day Vernon was part of West Northfield, Massachusetts; but naturally Vermont didn't exist as Vermont then anyway.

Our discoveries contradict what historians said.

All the relics we picked up after the flood come from the Vermont side. As we got on to the idea, we begun finding things, some that we could name and some that we couldn't. At first I saved them all, and the only thing that ever got away from me was copper beads. I would pick them up in my fingers and crumble them, before I found out what they were. They was old, oxidized sheet copper, rolled into little cylinders—trade copper that the Indians swapped skins for. The beads practically fall into powder if you touch them, and it was quite a while before I realized they wasn't just scrap copper.

Copper ornaments given the Indians by fur traders.

I wasn't expecting copper beads, either, because Gramp had told me that the Indians sometimes made beads from volcanic glass. When I found the pottery, I said to John Gale if they made pottery they must have made clay beads. I started looking.

John thought it would be quite a joke if I found a bead in thirty acres of sand.

I said, "I found a blue one, but I guess it's just an ordinary bead."

He said, "Save it." So I put it in my pocketbook. I said, "I found a white one."

He said, "Let's see it." So we started collecting beads.

Sifting for beads.

Next time, we brought down boxes with screening on the bottom. We would pick out some small obstruction on the ground, like a little root or stub, that water would swirl over in the flood, and where pebbles would collect. Anywhere they collected, I shoveled them up with a trowel and sifted the beads out on the screening.

One copper thing I found was a thunderbird. There's one carved on the rocks on the south bank of the mouth of the West River, too; it's under water now. All the Indians all over the country had the thunderbird. He was supposed to beat the air with his wings, and make it thunder, and when he winked it lightened. When they needed water in the dry country, they got out this bird and drummed up a little rain.

We hunted relics all the way up and down the river from Dummerston to the Massachusetts line, and in the end we got together quite a collection of different things: axes, knives, pottery, adzes, pestles.

Their knives.

A lot of the points that people call spear points are nothing more or less than knives. These points have a shank, and was put in a heft or stick the same as an arrow only bigger, and used as a knife. We found points made of hard red slate that had to come from York State; we found white ones, black ones, brown ones, yellow ones, and different sorts of traprock.

That gave me the idea of making some myself. I tried making them with metal, I tried it with a staghorn the same as the Indians done. I got so I could make as good an arrow point as you would see in any museum. But still you shake it up with some real ones, and you will know it's a phony. In making one with modern tools you don't get the flaking like they got it, because we just chip it off or hammer it out, whereas theirs was flaked off or cleaved off like a diamond cutter would cleave it. You have to have a perfect eye for the grain of the stone. Gramp might have been able to make one that would fool you; I can't.

Trying my hand at an arrowhead.

We found quite a number of pestles, and hammerstones by the bushel. I have asked everybody I could find what hammerstones was for; once I asked somebody down to Deerfield in the Historical Society. They have a large collection of pitted stones there.

I asked the man what they hammered with the hammerstones, and he give me a book on the subject. All I found out was that they didn't know as much about it as I did. Hammerstones is kind of a universal mystery; they're found all over the world from Japan to Scandinavia, but nobody knows what they was used for.

The unsolved mystery of the hammerstones.

The big ones, weighing probably forty pounds, we know about. The pits in them come from drilling. You set the butt of the drill in the pit of the stone, and held the work in your fingers while you run the bow with the other hand to turn the drill. Some smaller stones was used the other way around, held by hand to push down on the butt of the drill. All those pits are smooth.

153

But the hammerstone is pecked out. It has a pit about the size of the end of your little finger, pecked out round, but rough. Sometimes there is twin pits on opposite sides of a stone, as if they would eventually drill through it. There don't seem to be any special kind of stone, just any one of a size to hold in the palm of your hand. Some Indian things I can make a better guess about than a fellow in a museum that never worked with his hands, but the hammerstones have me beat.

If it hadn't been for the big flood of 1936, John and I wouldn't never have found a thing, because we hadn't learned where to dig. We found most of our relics anywhere from ten inches to two or three feet below the present ground level; it had been silted over or plowed over since it was occupied. We found everything below the black line—a thin line, probably not more than a quarter of an inch, but black in white sand. If you traced it back to where the bank had caved off, you could follow it all the way from the level we found the relics on. As I said before, by taking the black under a glass I discovered it was charcoal. After the topsoil was washed down to this black level, within a year or so it all come into wild clover, which is a sure sign of ashes.

Sure signs of lodge sites and campgrounds.

Now that I've learned how, I can pretty near count on going out and finding an Indian lodge site or campground whenever I want to. For one thing, the Indians never picked a place where they couldn't get clean fresh water, either a spring near by or a nice stream running into the Connecticut.

I find a spot that looks like good camping ground, with water, and then I begin hunting for burnt stones. The Indians would gather stones about the size of your fist, and bury them in the fire. Down on the flat at the bow of the river there was a lodge

that must have had three or four rooms, because there was a hearth in each. You can detect the firestones because they are burned to the color of brick.

These stones evidently served two purposes. If a man wanted to heat something right away, he just dropped these stones in it—probably picked them up with a piece of bark or two sticks. The other purpose, I finally made up my mind the reason for so many stones in a pile was that during the day they were piled in the fire and heated red hot. After the fire went down at night, the stones still threw out heat and warmed the lodge just the same.

Firestones for quick boiling, or heat at night.

Down on the flat, I heated one up and put it in a pail of water; it went in with quite a sizz. When I reached in and picked it out, I sure learned something. Put a four- or five-pound red-hot stone in a pail of water, and you will be very much surprised— the same as I was—how much heat it has to throw off before it will cool down enough so you can pick it up.

When the flood uncovered an Indian fire, the stones and the ashes and the charcoal would stay right there, just as if the fire hadn't been lit more than a year or two ago. Until I got used to finding one, I was never sure if a fire was left by some of my young in-laws from Vernon, or by the Indians that gave the name to Bloody Brook at South Deerfield in 1675.

The old trail across to the west side of Vermont went north as far as Bellows Falls, and then angled northwest—up streams, through Proctorsville Gulf, and over the height of land at Mount Holly—on to Lake Champlain. That was the path from east to west that the Indians followed when they raided Deerfield; on the way back they would go through Guilford, and John always wondered if his white arrow-point watch fob was one they lost on the way up.

I remember Gramp telling me the Indians never killed game that they didn't need to eat, but he said they was most always hungry anyway. And they never disturbed nut trees or berry vines or anything that would produce food.

Searching is fun, then give it away. It's funny, I put in most of my spare time Indian-relicking, but after I've found the stuff I don't care to have it all kicking around. I give most of it away. Maybe it's because Gramp taught me enough so that I could go out and live in the woods myself, if I had to. I could find things to eat, and make a bow and arrows, and some kind of stone tools, even if not as good as the Indians made. I have fun searching, but the actual things is no novelty to me; if I wanted some, I could make them.

That goes double for the old Indians themselves. We found various bones that we didn't know, and the only way I could tell legs from arms was to try

156

them on. John had a few of those, but he never saved any skulls.

One Sunday I was going along on the sand by the river, looking very close for points and beads and things, when I saw what I concluded must be the top of a skull showing in the sand. It was yellowed over, just a nice medium bald-headed size. I was kind of gazing around for other things, but I reached down to try the skull carefully and see if it was buried so deep that I should have to dig to get it out. I put my hand on it, and I don't know how far I jumped; ten feet, probably. It was hot and soft: a rotten grapefruit rind.

We meet the guardian of a lodge.

But we did find one old Indian, sitting waiting. He was on the New Hampshire shore, and his lodge wasn't too far away; there was a spring a short distance off, and I dug one or two arrow points out of the place where his lodge had been.

We was fishing, and went over to the spring after a drink, and I discovered one of those firestones they had in their lodges, so I started looking around.

The bank had caved down and overhung a little, and I looked up under the bank. I discovered this Indian, this skeleton, sitting under there, folded up with his head between his knees and his hands down around his feet. He was about the sorriest-looking skeleton I've ever seen. I looked all around to see if they'd buried any of his personal property with him, but he didn't have no more than when he was born.

We caved the bank down over him, and left him. I guess he'll probably stay there until the Great Spirit digs him up again.

THE AUTHORS

Walter Needham is a Vermonter whose forebears settled in the state in 1794, and he is the grandson of Leroy L. Bond—the "Gramp" of *A Book of Country Things*. Mr. Needham's vivid memories of this man born in a log cabin, who served in the Civil War, who could do anything with his hands from making bullets to building a stone wall—above all, who lived all his life in the self-reliant ways of frontier America—are a direct link between that colonial America and the space age.

Now a grandfather himself, Walter Needham is as busy as ever with his work and his hobbies, in keeping with the Yankee theory that "it's better to wear out than to rust out."

Barrows Mussey—linguist, author, and former publisher—recorded Walter Needham's talk about Grandpa's ideas and customs when the Musseys lived near the Needhams in Guilford. He has translated some sixty books, so it follows that his presentation of this narrative faithfully retains the individuality of the speaker.

Mr. Mussey is also recognized as an authority on early Americana, and among the books he has written are *Young Father Time, a Yankee Portrait* (of Eli Terry), *Old New England,* and *Vermont Heritage.* He is the editor of *Yankee Life by Those Who Lived It.*

INDEX

161